THE SCIENCE
OF HAPPINESS

THE SCIENCE OF HAPPINESS

Seven Lessons for Living Well

BRUCE HOOD

ROWMAN & LITTLEFIELD
Lanham • Boulder • New York • London

Published by Rowman & Littlefield
An imprint of The Rowman & Littlefield Publishing Group, Inc.
4501 Forbes Boulevard, Suite 200, Lanham, Maryland 20706
www.rowman.com

86-90 Paul Street, London EC2A 4NE, United Kingdom

British Library Cataloguing in Publication Information Available

Library of Congress Cataloging-in-Publication Data Available

ISBN 9798881803575 (paper : alk. paper) | ISBN 9798881803582 (ebook)

♾™ The paper used in this publication meets the minimum requirements of American
National Standard for Information Sciences—Permanence of Paper for Printed Library
Materials, ANSI/NISO Z39.48-1992.

This book is dedicated to all the students and colleagues I have had the good fortune to work with over the years who have taught me so much.

CONTENTS

Preface

Have you noticed how happy most young children are? They seem to delight in the simplest things. Puddles, dirt, snow, twigs. At the back of my office is a junior school playground. Every break, it is filled with the laughter and squeals of young children at play. Where does all that joy go? We start off *happy* as young children but many of us turn into *unhappy* adults, dissatisfied with our lives. Even when things are going well for us, genuine and sustained happiness can feel elusive. Why is this, and what, if anything, can be done about it?

I've been studying children for four decades as a developmental psychologist. I am fascinated by the processes that take us from a helpless baby, dependent on others for survival, to an adult capable of painting the Sistine Chapel, composing symphonies, building spaceships or waging war. My life has been dedicated to research and teaching my students to inspire them to become the next generation of scientists. This has been immensely satisfying for most of my career, but about six years ago, I noticed that each new intake of students was increasingly unhappy and anxious about their academic performance. They worried excessively about their grades. They wanted more instruction about how to go about the various assessments. They seemed less interested by the amazing discoveries in the field that they were learning about and more focused on how to get the top marks. My joy and enthusiasm for teaching students had been undermined by a pragmatic, goal-directed approach that was accompanied by a rising tide of misery and unhappiness. Of course these ambitions for academic achievement are admirable goals, but not at the cost of personal happiness. It wasn't just my students. The whole sector of higher education was experiencing an epidemic of mental health problems. The transition to university has always been a challenging time. I know because I wrote about it in my first happiness research paper over thirty years ago, but things are much worse today.[1] Students were overly preoccupied with their own poor mental health and I had to do something about it.

I knew that there was a field within my discipline called *positive psychology* that sought to improve mental well-being through simple routines and activities. I was sceptical. I heard that meditation was very effective, but it had its roots in Eastern religion rather than evidence-based science. There were countless articles in the media on how to be happy and successful that seemed to me to be quick fixes. How could they improve happiness so easily? Airport bookstores were crammed with self-help books often written by 'experts' with questionable credentials. Positive psychology all sounded a bit too much like hype and rather wishy-washy to me, but I was willing to give it a go.

By coincidence, I discovered that a former Harvard student of mine, Laurie Santos, a senior academic psychologist and head of a residential college at Yale, had created a well-being course, 'Psychology and the Good Life', that had become the most popular class on campus. In her typical generous and selfless manner, Santos sent me her notes, to which I added my spin to create 'The Science of Happiness' course that I piloted in 2018 at the University of Bristol. I wasn't sure if anyone would come. As it happens, over 500 people, students and staff, turned up on the first day. What makes this extra-remarkable was that this pilot was not an official university unit for credit, but simply a series of weekly lunchtime lectures anyone could attend.

Since my course was about the scientific approach to under-standing happiness, I included studies that sought to explain human behaviour in terms of the underlying mechanisms in the brain. My own areas of interest – child development, the self and neuroscience – played central roles. I wanted to share my passion for the power of data and evidence, so I included lectures on statistics and experimental design to demonstrate how science is the best way to discover truths in the world. Unlike many positive psychology advocates, I was cautious not to oversell the promise of the principles I was teaching. I was determined to approach the Science of Happiness as rigorously as possible, so I had the audience participate in psychometric tests before and after the course to determine whether the recommended activities made any difference to their happiness. I informed them that they were taking part in their own experiment and the outcome would determine the future of the course. And I promised: if it didn't work, I would abandon the course and return to my studies.

After the course was over, the student feedback was extremely positive. They found it interesting and fun, and enjoyed the opportunities to participate. For some members of the audience, the experience had been 'transformative'. But what would the data say about their happiness? I remember tentatively running the psychometric scores through the statistical analysis, and I was absolutely *gobsmacked* by the results. Overall, on all the measures of well-being that I had administered, there was what we call a highly significant 10–15 per cent increase in positive scores from before the course began until it ended ten weeks later. That may not sound like a transformation into a state of eternal happiness and bliss, but this degree of change, over a relatively short period of time, is meaningful. I was now a convert. I knew then that you can make people happier through science, and through education. Making you happier is the purpose of this book.

Introduction

As a scientist, I always want to know the answer to the 'why' questions. Why do some of us feel unhappy? Why is happiness so fragile? And why do positive psychology interventions work? I think the answers can be found in childhood.

In most families, young children are the centre of attention. They have not yet encountered the competitive world of social relationships and the acute sense of being evaluated or judged by others that makes up most of life by the time you reach adolescence. Most young children are happily self-centred, or egocentric, living in the present moment with little room for regrets about the past or worries for the future.

However, as children grow up and enter the competitive worlds of school exams, relationships, social media and work, they find they are no longer the centre of attention. They must learn to get on with others who are also vying for status and recognition. Conflicts often arise when both parties fail to appreciate the other's perspective. We want to have status and be admired by others, but this too leads to conflict. It is difficult to be both a winner and a team player at the same time. You can't be the most popular person without others being less popular. You can't be the most liked person without others being disliked. You can't be the most successful without others failing – at least, according to the egocentric view. In order to get along with others and become accepted into society, we need to appreciate what others might be thinking and consider how we should act with this in mind, but it does take some practice and skill. These abilities emerge over childhood.

By the time we enter adulthood we have accumulated more cares and worries than our younger selves. So, when we are trapped in our own self-centred universe – which happens often – it's easy for that self-focus to become directed towards our problems and we can blow everything out of proportion. Consider a representation of our ego in relation to others, the problems we face and the exchange of points of view (Fig. I.1).

Fig. I.1: Representation of an overly egocentric social network

When we are egocentric, we are dominant at the centre of our universe and perceive relationships as tending to go in one direction. We impact on others and when others impact on us there is little mutual exchange because we tend not to take the other's perspective into consideration. Unlike children, egocentric adults are very much aware of present and potential future problems. We view our problems as bigger than they really are. We don't appreciate that others have their own problems, or if they do, then they do not compare to our own. As far as we are concerned, the difficulties we face are the most important.

But there is another way that we can see the world: from an *other*-centred, or *allocentric* view, which can lead to greater happiness. An allocentric view considers the perspectives of others and the interconnectedness of the social world (Fig. I.2).

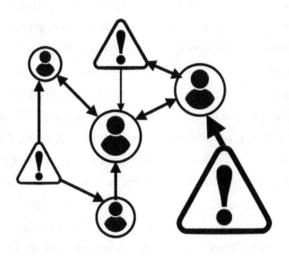

Fig. I.2: Representation of an allocentric social network

Our self is reduced and now comparable to others. Our relationships are more reciprocal, and we are aware that there are issues that impact on others that are more important to them than our problems are to us. This view puts issues into perspective and often makes our own concerns seem less burdensome. As the saying goes, 'A problem shared is a problem halved.' When we think and behave more allocentrically, we benefit from the social support we receive and the unexpected happiness that can be found by reaching out to others.

Most adults can step out of their ego and take an allocentric perspective when they need to. After all, learning to do so is an important part of growing up, but it is difficult to think like this spontaneously. We are seldom aware of the difficulties others face unless they are close to us, or their plight is specifically brought to our attention, because we are so caught up in our own world-view. Even when we do hear of others' problems, when we are too egocentric there is still a tendency to regard them as less important than our own.

As the Greek Stoic philosopher Epictetus said, 'It's not what happens to you, but how you respond, that matters.' In other words, two people could face the same negative life event but one will brush it off and the other will ruminate for days. Why is that? What makes someone see a glass half-full as opposed to a glass half-empty? Why are some of us happier than others? Are we born that way, or do we become like that?

It's true that happy kids tend to grow up into happy adults. What makes a happy kid is partly down to the genes we inherit from our parents. By measuring happiness in both identical twins who share all their genes and non-identical twins who share half of the same genes, scientists can work out what proportion of the variation in scores comes down to biology and what comes from the environment. This is called *heritability*, and when measures of well-being are compared, on average no more than 40–50 per cent of the differences and similarities comes down to genes[1] – an estimate that is not too different to that for intelligence.[2] We each inherit a proportion of our dispositions, both good and bad, from our parents, but not all of them. Happiness, like other aspects of personality, can't all be explained by biology.

The UK Office for National Statistics interviewed groups of youngsters aged ten to fifteen years of age and asked them what made them happy.[3] It wasn't their PlayStation, number of Instagram followers, money, holidays or doing well at school. 'Feeling loved and having positive, supportive relationships, particularly with friends and family, including having someone to talk to and rely on' was consistently stated as a top priority for children to have a happy life. This is important as another survey, of over 17,000 adults born in 1970, which asked the question 'How dissatisfied or satisfied are you about the way your life has turned out so far?',[4] found that the biggest predictor of an individual's adult satisfaction at forty-two years of age was how well adjusted they were as children in terms of emotional health. Our social interactions as children lay down the foundations of how we behave as adults, and that, in turn, impacts on our happiness. When we are connected to others, we learn how to cope better with life's setbacks and challenges. Of all the things in the environment that might contribute to satisfaction with life, such as salaries, marriage or romantic partners, it's how well we got on with others as children that is the biggest predictor of our well-being as adults.

Does this mean that if we had an unhappy childhood, we can't be happy adults? Not necessarily. My own childhood was unhappy. I was raised in an itinerant family, constantly moving from one country to another because of an abusive, unhappy, alcoholic father seeking employment, purpose and meaning in his life. He died when I was fifteen, leaving me to fend for myself after my mother returned to her native Australia two years later. In spite of this traumatic childhood, I regard myself as a relatively happy adult. I don't know why this is the case, but I do know it is possible to make people happier through education and I have the evidence to back that up.[5]

This evidence comes from my 'Science of Happiness' lecture series, which has been running now for the past five years at the University of Bristol as a credit-bearing course for first-year fresher students.[6] Since teaching the course, I have come to realise that there is a common mechanism at work in childhood that might provide answers to the 'why' questions of happiness. Our egocentric bias may always be with us, but we can train ourselves to think more allocentrically. Attaining this balance between egocentrism and allocentrism is crucial to this process and at the core of each of the practical takeaways in this book.

Over seven lessons I want to explain how to pursue happiness using evidence-based techniques, but I also want to explain why they work. Lesson One, 'Alter Your Ego', will explain how our sense of self is constructed during the course of child development. We begin with a very egocentric self but become increasingly aware of others and our place in society. If we remain dominantly egocentric, then there is a danger that this self-focus will distort our perspectives and lead to unhappiness. In Lesson Two, 'Avoid Isolation', we discover how humans became so socially dependent due to our unusual childhoods and large brains. The brain is also the topic of Lesson Three, 'Reject Negative Comparisons', where we demonstrate the inherent biases in the way we process information and how these biases can get in the way of our happiness. In Lesson Four, 'Become More Optimistic', we address the problem of our tendency to focus on and assume the worst. We expand on this in Lesson Five, 'Control Your Attention', which explores how, when we are not concentrating or engaged in activities that require our attention, our minds wander towards negative thoughts. To combat this tendency, Lesson Six, 'Connect With Others', reveals the benefits of interacting with others and the misconceived awkwardness we think will occur when we speak to strangers. And finally, in Lesson Seven, 'Get Out of Your Own Head', we explore different ways to see the world in a new light, to improve our happiness.

The Science of Happiness is more than a self-help book. In many ways, it is a *self-destruct* book, because the overly egocentric self can be the source of so much unhappiness. However, we cannot and should not try to remove our self-perspective by becoming solely allocentric. If we only think and feel for others, then we are in danger of entirely losing our sense of self, which is just as important for our mental well-being as our connection with others. If we focus on conflicts and crises that are beyond our power to change, we are going to be overwhelmed with despair. We should not become so dependent on others for our own happiness that we lose total control over our own mental well-being.

Across the seven lessons, you will learn that a balance needs to be struck between our egocentric viewpoint and adopting a more allocentric perspective. Throughout and at the end of each lesson, there will be simple exercises to help you with this shift to becoming more balanced – and therefore happier.

But remember, knowledge is simply not enough. We have repeatedly shown that our course improves students' mental well-being and reduces their feelings of anxiety and loneliness, but the improvement lasts only as long as the students keep up their practices.[7] It's like physical health: you can be fitter, but only so long as you work at it. If you stop living a healthier lifestyle, then you will stop being healthy. The same is true of happiness. You need to work at it, to *practise* happiness, in order to achieve the lasting benefits.

LESSON ONE

Alter Your Ego

It used to be thought that Earth was at the centre of the universe, with the Sun and Moon orbiting our planet. That all changed in the sixteenth century, when Copernicus explained the movements of the planets, subsequently verified by the observations of Galileo with his telescope. This revelation produced a paradigm shift – a radical rethinking of our place in the universe. What is true of the cosmos is true of each of us. We are not the centre of the universe, even though we may think so. If we wish to be happier, we too must undergo a radical rethink in our own lives. We must abandon our notion of a self-centred universe with our ego at the middle, surrounded by others, and recognise our place and how we relate to each other. As described in the introduction, we must shift from an overly egocentric view to one which is more *other*-focused, or *allocentric*.

Radically rethinking ourselves in order to grow happier is challenging because we all start with a rampantly egocentric view of the world. This arises due to the nature of conscious-ness and the way we begin to process the world as children. When we acknowledge our bias to observe everything from this egocentric perspective, then we can start to change our perception. By recognising and increasing our allocentric view, we can reduce the burden of the problems and concerns we bring upon ourselves and benefit from the support and objec-tivity that social interactions can provide.

Children usually make this transition as part of normal development, but we all vary in how much we make that change. The reason that this shift is necessary is because our adult happiness depends on it. As we noted in the Introduction, happy children grow up to be happy adults, and it's our social connections that make us happy as children. But if we want to get on with others, then we must become less self-centred and more allocentric. The roots of our adult happiness can be found in our childhoods.

In this first lesson, I want to introduce the concept of the self and how it emerges over childhood as we develop interaction with others. We are so used to the word 'self' that we rarely think about how it is used in different ways to refer to differ-ent things. Our self is who we are, but who we are depends on the context. If I ask you at an interview to tell me a bit about yourself, then the expectation is that you are going to give me a potted history of your work experience, skills and training. If we are on a date, and I ask you to tell me about yourself, then I don't expect a résumé but, rather, your likes and dis-likes, political views, favourite foods and music. Then there is another sense of self, which is the mental life we experience. Occasionally, I may sense a distortion in consciousness and say,

'I am not myself.' The autobiographical facts about me have not changed but, rather, I feel that I am different in some way. In effect, the self is constantly constructed from the combination of a conscious appraisal and a history of personal experiences.

The nineteenth-century philosopher William James drew a useful distinction between the 'I-self' – the conscious actor, knower and thinker – as distinct from the 'Me-self' – the objective story of one's actions, knowledge and thoughts.[1] Let me illustrate the difference between the I-self and Me-self by asking you a question. Which flavour of ice cream do you prefer – vanilla or chocolate? Take a moment to consider. In answering, let me point out different aspects of the self that you may not have thought about. First, you have an experience of conscious awareness. As you were reading the sentence, your inner voice spoke the words, you understood the question and began to formulate an answer. That conscious awareness is the I-self, the actor. This is the inner mental world that we are aware of. This is where thoughts and emotions are experienced. But this conscious I-self draws upon a library of knowledge where an unconscious Me-self resides, the story of who we are. To answer the ice-cream question, you must retrieve the relevant information from memory, which keeps a record of your personal history of eating frozen dairy delights. This is the Me-self repository of knowledge. Although distinguishable, the I-self and the Me-self both feed into the construct that we call 'self'. In other words, conscious experiences become memories and memories can re-enter our conscious experiences on recall.

When our stream of conscious thought appears organised, coherent, unified, enduring, with a sense of agency and free will, then we experience the self that most of us are all familiar with, but it doesn't follow that a self exists a priori or independently to its constituent components. This is why I have described the self as an illusion.[2] I am not denying there is an experience of self, but it's not what it seems. Illusions are the same: they appear to be one thing, when they are another.

'Hold on one moment,' you say, 'not so fast. Who is searching for an answer to the ice-cream question if not the self?' This would seem to create a paradox – the self is both monitoring experiences and generated by experiences. Like the hands in the Escher lithograph, one creates the other (see below).

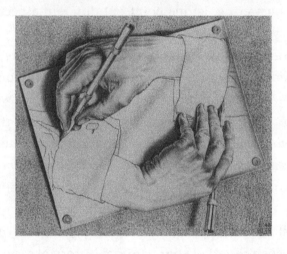

This paradox exists only if you consider the I-self as independent and the antecedent or initiator of thoughts and actions. And it doesn't depend on constant consciousness, either. If consciousness is absent – and we experience this every night when we are in deep, dreamless sleep – then the self reassembles every morning when we awaken. At first, the I-self becomes aware, and then we rummage through our Me-self to fill in the agenda for the day. It will not – and cannot – be the same self as the one from the previous day, though we rarely notice any difference, and it changes with each subsequent day of experience, but it is a self resketched, nonetheless. This is not a new idea. One translation of the Buddha's *Dhammapada* reads, 'What we are today comes from our thoughts of yesterday, and our present thoughts build our life of tomorrow: our life is the creation of our mind.'[3]

We are not normally aware of these different components of the constructed self until they become disconnected. Consider the plight of Clive Wearing, who is unable to form new memories, or at least become aware of them.[4] In 1985, Wearing was an eminent Cambridge University musicologist who was struck down with *herpes simplex* encephalitis, an infection of the brain, which destroyed his capacity to store any new memories. Wearing has profound anterograde amnesia, which means that anything he experiences anew is lost within seconds. He remembers many skills acquired prior to his illness, such as how to play the piano and what his wife Deborah looks like, but he cannot remember anything new that happens to him.

Since his illness, Wearing has updated a diary every day in an effort to make sense of his life. Most of the entries consist of variations of the same sentence, underscored and repeated from page to page: 'Now I am awake' with the time of entry, 10:30; 'I am awake', but then scored out ~~10:30 'I am awake,'~~ with each successive entry, 10:32 'Now I am truly awake!'

His memory lasts for about seven seconds. In terms of self-hood, Wearing is unable to update the Me-self and integrate this with the conscious subjective awareness of the I-self.

Hence, he experiences an absence of continuity or any enduring self. Wearing is locked in his own perpetual *Groundhog Day* – the 1993 film that tells the story of a man who relives the same day over and over again.

At this point in a book on happiness, you might ask: 'Why all the focus and philosophical musings about the self? Is this really necessary? This is all a bit too abstract. I just want to be happier.' But if we want to change for the better, then we need to understand the true nature of the self, how it is constructed and how it can change, because we can't truly become happier without a better understanding of ourselves. We are so wedded to our experience of self that we believe that it stands apart from experience and distant from others. Like an observer upon the world, rather than constructed from the world, we view our self as separate. We don't even believe we will change as we grow older, even though most of us acknowledge that we have changed since childhood. The assumption that we have reached the endpoint of our own development is called the 'end of history illusion'.[5]

The truth is you can – and probably will – change as your self rewrites itself through experiences. If you want to be happier, you need to take this opportunity to see yourself as the product of your interconnectedness with others and not as an isolated island.

When do I begin?

Most psychologists agree that the self is gradually constructed over childhood as the combination of greater understanding and personal memories. Indeed, the twentieth-century Swiss developmental psychologist Jean Piaget claimed that the infant starts off with no appreciation of self as distinct from the external world.[6] Rather, newborns experience the world as an extension of their own minds. They are in a state of extreme *solipsism* (from the Latin for 'alone' and 'self'). When you experience extreme solipsism, the distinction between self and the world disappears. This is also what happens when you're on a psychedelic trip, which we will discuss in the last lesson.

Though newborns are extremely egocentric, they are attuned to the presence of significant others, especially the mother. The early years tend to be sociable ones. Babies prefer to stare at the human face more than other patterns,[7] especially the face of their mother.[8] In turn, we love to look at our babies and treat them as little adults. Doting parents typically treat their newborn babies as independent little persons with their own personalities and the full range of mental states.[9] This informs how we talk to and interact with babies. We make comments like, 'Oh, you are so funny!' or 'Are you being naughty?' Such interactions stimulate the emergence of *intersubjectivity* – an appreciation of the self as separate but in relation to others.

It is only a matter of weeks before the young infant is initiating and participating in behaviours that forge and strengthen the bonds of social connection. Take smiling, for example. Many parents report that their newborn baby smiles at them. In many cases, they are instead grimacing with gastric wind, but within six weeks most babies will purposefully smile back at you. This *social smiling* marks a significant milestone in self-development – an example of intersubjectivity that signals the beginning of social communication. If you look directly at a two-month-old, in most cases they will stare intensely back at you and smile. If you smile back, they smile more, and you both end up laughing! If you look away, they stop smiling.[10] Brain-imaging studies reveal that the reward centres of the brain light up when young mothers are presented with images of their babies smiling but not when they are frowning.[11] If someone smiles at us and we smile back, not only does that signal that we are paying attention to them, but that we are socially engaging with them in a positive way. Imagine how you would feel if you smiled at someone and they either didn't respond, turned away or frowned back at you. I expect you would feel a little crestfallen. At this young age, social smiling is a strategy babies unwittingly employ to find out who likes them. Initially they smile at everyone but over time they become more selective. By the end of the first year, most are now fearful of strangers.[12] This reflects a growing awareness of others and a strengthening of the bonds we form with family.

We will examine in more detail how these early emotional attachments form in the next lesson, as they play an important role in shaping our future adult relationships. However, suffice to say, happiness depends on forging bonds with those we can trust; babies come to rely on those who behave consistently towards them. One of the best ways to build a reliable understanding of others is to establish a rapport. Babies send out signals that adults can respond to and the adults who are the most responsive get the babies' attention.[13] This is a good strategy – to focus their efforts on those who are the most invested in them. When others are inconsistent or unreliable, babies do not easily form stable attachments.[14] This is also true of adults who want to establish worthwhile relationships.[15] Unpredictable people can be a waste of time. If someone doesn't turn up or is late for a date, then you can miss out on the meal or the movie screening that you wanted to attend. Tardiness also sends a signal of how important you are to them. If someone can't be bothered to turn up on time, they may be disorganised, or it may be an indication that they don't consider their appointment with you a priority. Inconsistency is also a negative parenting flaw because children cannot build reliable personal attachments when people are unpredictable. This creates tension, anxiety and leads to unstable emotional attachment among children. But not all is lost, as parents trained to consider their child's attentional signals through video feedback can learn to build better, more stable attachment styles.[16]

The behaviour of young babies suggests that they are sociable creatures wired to interact with others from the start. Clearly, there are many ways in which babies appear to be prosocial. These social behaviours are an evolved strategy to maximise the support and care from others and build bonds with those who are most likely to look after them. Babies clearly recognise and enjoy the attention of family members, but they are still at the centre of their egocentric universe. They haven't yet learned to be allocentric. Over time, these relationships will extend beyond the immediate caregivers and eventually out to other people, and that is when they must develop their allocentric sense of self, one that is interconnected with others.

Happy childhood memories?

For most of us, watching babies at play is a happy experience. They seem so cute and innocent, and it is hard to resist their appeal. Very few of us can be indifferent to their charms. Clearly the human infant is already a skilled social operator, manipulating adults, but given their minimal experience, they haven't yet formed a Me-self. They are living in the joyful moment of self-centred attention, oblivious to much else. No one can remember the day we awoke with a sudden awareness of self and our standing in the world. Surveys of hundreds of individuals reveal that most of us, if we're honest, have little memory of ourselves before our second birthday. It's not that our memories have faded over the decades – for example, seventy-year-olds can remember many more events from fifty years earlier than twenty-year-olds can from being a baby only eighteen years previously.[17] Prior to around two years of age, all that most people can report are sporadic impressions or events, such as a bird flying in through the window when they were lying in the crib (my wife's earliest memory). I have no such recollections. During the second to third year, however, our childhood memories take on a quality that makes them more autobiographical than the unconnected episodes of earlier infancy. This is when the Me-self starts to form.

Biological explanations for this *infantile amnesia* are based on the maturation of the hippocampus, the structure deep within the brain most closely associated with long-term memories.[18] It's the structure that was damaged by the *herpes simplex* infection that destroyed Wearing's capacity to encode new memories. Memories are stories that involve us – the actor. We experience the events from an entirely personal perspective. The origins of autobiographical memory are likely to first require an independent self as the protagonist within the context of the experience, in the same way that we need a central character in a story to make sense of the structure of events. Without an enduring, independent sense of self, it is impossible to form autobiographical memories. This would explain why children whose caregivers talk to them more frequently about the past have much better early childhood memories when they are older. These conversations help to structure early memories into meaningful, coherent events with the child at the centre.[19]

One of the earliest pieces of evidence for a slowly emerging self-awareness comes from appreciating one's own reflection in the mirror. When presented with a mirror, young human infants initially treat their reflected image as another child, but at around twenty to twenty-four months they begin to show reliable mirror identification, indicating a new level of self-awareness.[20] This is one reason why such self-recognition coincides with the formation of the first reports of autobiographical memories. With a protagonist in place, we can start to construct the memories into coherent stories that are more organised and thus more easily encoded – and so the I-self and Me-self begin to work together.[21]

The egocentric child

Even as the sense of a self starts to emerge and strengthen, the child still fails to understand the true nature of reality as distinct from what they perceive. Piaget's description of the egocentric child, observing and interpreting the world from their own perspective, still holds today.[22] For example, if you pour the contents of a glass into another-shaped container that is taller, young children think the volume of liquid has changed. It looks different to the child, so they reason that the volumes are now different.

The classic demonstration of egocentrism is Piaget's Three Mountains task.[23] In that experiment, children sit across from an adult at a table with a set of three papier mâché mountains in front of them, each with a different landmark like a building or a tree. When asked to choose from a number of photographs taken from different angles around the table, egocentric children can easily select the picture that corresponds to the arrangement of the three mountains from where they are sitting. However, if asked to select the photograph that corresponds to the view that the adult has, from a different perspective across the table, the egocentric child typically selects the same photograph that represents their own perspective. Again, they assume that others experience the same viewpoint as their own. If you play hide-and-seek with an egocentric child, then don't be too surprised if they try to hide by running to the corner of the room and pulling a towel over their head, thinking that if they can't see you, then it stands to reason that you can't see them (Fig. 1.1).[24]

Fig. 1.1: A miserable fail at hide-and-seek.
(Permission: Elizabeth Bonawitz)

It's not that young children *can't* think from another perspective. Various studies show that children can think more
allocentrically if you deliberately draw their attention to a different perspective.[25] Rather, egocentrism is the default mode of
thought for young children that they must learn to overcome
to be accepted by others. Indeed, egocentric thinking represents a considerable obstacle in communication. If you ever
listen to a couple of pre-schoolers in conversation, they might
as well not be talking to one another.

'I have a tricycle.'

'So what? When I grow up, I am going to be a policeman.'

'It's blue.'

'I want to be just like my dad.'

It's not that young children don't care about others but,
rather, they cannot easily imagine another's perspective. When

a child under the age of four is asked to imagine what another person might be thinking, they typically respond that others have exactly the same thoughts as they do. If you ask a three-year-old what's inside a tube of Smarties, they are likely to answer 'Smarties'.[26] If you show the child that the tube actually contains pencils, they find that amusing (some kids are easily amused). But if you then ask them what they thought was in the tube originally, they'll say 'pencils' – as if they have conveniently rewritten history to fit with what they now know to be true. These children don't seem to recognise or admit that they were initially mistaken (and we all know a few adults like that!). But what is more surprising is that if you ask them what another child who hasn't yet seen the contents will answer in response to the same question, they say that the other child will reply 'pencils'. They believe that the other child knows what they themselves now know to be true. Again, because they are so egocentric, they expect others to be able to read what's on their mind.

We can imagine what someone else is thinking by putting ourselves in their shoes. We can simulate a theory of what they may be thinking based on our past experiences, similar circumstances or what we predict they might be thinking. We operate with a *theory of mind*.[27] It is a mentalising skill that develops over childhood and plays a critical role in our capacity for social interaction.

As one of the demonstrations for my televised BBC 2011 Royal Institution Christmas Lectures on the brain, I asked two children from the audience, Mark and Olivia, both about eight years of age, to act out a theory of mind scenario. Olivia was asked to leave while I showed Mark a cabinet that I wheeled out in front of the audience. On top of the cabinet were a brown box and a green box, each with a lid. I handed Mark a model of the brain and asked him to put it in the brown box while I continued talking. After a minute, I asked Mark to retrieve the brain, whereupon he opened the brown box, where he last saw it to discover it was missing. He then opened the green box, where the model had been moved to. With his mature object concept, he knew it must be somewhere. When asked, Mark assumed there must be some trapdoor mechanism, but what he didn't know was that a diminutive magician, Billy Kidd, was crouched, hidden inside the cabinet making the switch. That was odd and a little amusing for the audience, but there was no thunderous applause.

Fig. 1.2: Theory of mind demonstration. (Permission: Author)

I then asked Mark what he thought Olivia would do when presented with the scenario. Armed with his theory of mind, Mark was able to predict that Olivia would also search in the brown box first where she last saw it placed because she couldn't know about Billy Kidd. For dramatic effect, however, we decided to change the climax. This time Billy Kidd wore a rubber monster hand to grab Olivia when she opened the green box. After Olivia had opened the first empty box, the audience could see what was going to happen next and became increasingly excited. Each audience member was using their own theory of mind to predict the surprise that the unsuspecting Olivia was going to get. When Olivia jumped back in fright from the grasping monster hand, the audience exploded into squeals of delight and applause. By predicting what was going to happen, the anticipation had amplified the comic effect.

Just about all our social interactions, especially with strangers or in uncertain situations, require a theory of mind. However, without a theory of mind, if you're someone who believes that others think the same thoughts as you and see the world the same way as you, then that is going to present some considerable obstacles when you try to interact with them – not only as children but as adults as well. That lack of insight impacts on our opportunities to find happiness. For example, as we will discover in Lesson Six, one of the best ways to generate happiness is to strike up a conversation with a stranger, but most of us shun the opportunity because we think that this will be awkward and that the other person will be thinking the same thing – when in fact the opposite is true.

Who am I?

At between two and four years of age, the I-self combines with a Me-self that is becoming more elaborated with experiences and information about who we are: 'Who am I and which groups do I belong to?' The Me-self begins to fill up with relevant information. The leading psychologist in the child development of self, Susan Harter, identified four attributes that pre-schoolers typically use when describing their self. These are physical ('I have brown eyes'), activity ('I like to play football'), social ('I have a younger sister') and psychological ('I am happy').[28] These factoids are often very specific and unrelated. Children at this age also tend to be overly positive when describing themselves. As adults, we sometimes embellish our achievements when we want to impress another, but that's nothing in comparison to young children. They are unrealistically confident about their abilities ('I am very strong') and when tested, pre-schoolers invariably overestimate their performance on how far they can jump or accurately throw a ball. Again, this reflects an overly egocentric self.

The reason that young children are overly confident is that they don't compare themselves with others. Rather, they tend to compare themselves with how they were last week, so they are aware of their improvement and see this as positive progress. How ironic that we lose this tendency when we grow older, and that this loss can be the source of so much grief. Adults who fail to see personal progress tend to compare themselves with others rather than how they were doing one or five years ago – a preoccupation we will discuss in greater depth in Lesson Three, on the comparing brain.

In the early years of school children are still overly positive about their own abilities but they are becoming increasingly aware of others' opinions. There is a notable shift in their sense of self towards being more objective and considering themselves compared with their classmates. They are making more accurate comparisons but there is also a growing awareness of the importance of being accepted and not rejected by peers. For example, you see many more examples of altruistic behaviour such as sharing, but this is typically directed towards peers;[29] only later does helping others become less strategic. There is also an increasing interest in group identity, with prejudice starting to rear its ugly head around this age. Between five and seven years of age, children show strong preferences for their own racial group and prejudice against another group, especially if they have been raised in a segregated environment where they don't mix with other races on a regular basis.[30]

As children enter later childhood, around eight to ten years of age, their earlier exuberant positive self-assessments change to more accurate and often more negative evaluations, as they increasingly draw comparisons with peers.[31] They can recognise that they have both strengths and weaknesses, compared with the all-or-nothing mind of the younger child. They are now much less egocentric and more attuned to how they compare with others. Pride and shame are used to describe achievements independently of what parents are telling them. Increasingly, cultural norms and susceptibility to media portrayals are beginning to shape aspirations. Children at this age also begin to formulate idealised versions of what they would like to be. They are also much more likely to describe themselves in relational terms to their peers. Those who feel inferior can start to make downward comparisons with less gifted peers as a self-enhancement strategy to maintain their self-esteem.

Good job!

It is worth taking a moment to consider happiness as it relates to children's self-esteem. Self-esteem is the value that individuals place on themselves and is strongly associated with happiness. This association is not too surprising; it is difficult to feel happy if you do not feel worthy. Low self-esteem has been blamed for all manner of subsequent societal problems, including poor mental health, substance abuse, crime and violence. Since the 1970s and especially in the USA, there has been a movement to raise children's self-esteem as a preventive strategy against societal problems by raising educational performance. When I worked as a developmental psychologist in the USA, I was surprised how often the exclamation 'Good job!' was used by just about everyone interacting with children. It didn't really matter whether the child had done a good job or not. Rather, it had become second nature to constantly praise children to make them feel happier. Although the self-esteem movement has had considerable impact in both parenting and educational circles, the evidence to support the assumption that raising happiness by boosting self-esteem has beneficial outcomes is lacking.

Children regarded as having high self-esteem are rated as more confident, active, curious and independent.[32] They are also more able to cope with change. In contrast, children described as having low self-esteem tend to be withdrawn, lacking in confidence and not able to cope with challenges, instead getting frustrated quickly or giving up. What's interesting is that even though low- and high-esteem children differ in confidence, there are no actual differences in competence at this early age. It's not until they become more skilled, later in childhood, that the link between competence and confidence becomes established. This suggests that in early childhood, it is the adult input, mostly from caregivers, that instils confidence, but nonetheless children do become more attuned to objective performance measures with age – noting more how others are getting on compared with themselves. Children are not stupid; they know when they have done well, and this knowledge makes them happier.

Of course, you could argue that one begets the other; confidence increases the likelihood of children taking on more challenging roles, thereby improving performance that, in turn, increases confidence. On the other hand, a less confident child's performance could stagnate or drop off if they do not cope well with setbacks or push themselves. But this is a chicken-and-egg problem. Does confidence increase performance or is it the other way around? There is a clue in the order of change between self-esteem and performance. One tends to precede the other, suggesting a causal role. The evidence indicates that self-esteem rises after there is an increase in performance, and not the other way round.[33] Therefore unwarranted praise is not what drives increased performance.

When it comes to parenting styles connected to children's performance, three broad categories can be distinguished: *authoritative, authoritarian* and *permissive*.[34] Authoritative parents tend to be engaged in their child's performance. They may be firm and structured, but they are also warm and child-centred – a style of parenting that is associated with higher self-esteem.[35] In contrast, authoritarian parents are much stricter in controlling the situation and tend to dominate, stepping in and taking over without allowing the child to come up with solutions – a style of parenting that is associated with lower self-esteem.[36] This has sometimes been called 'helicoptering' – where the parent hovers over the child, looking for the first mishap to correct. Children of authoritarian parents tend to become overly dependent on others and think that others are responsible for their situation. Finally, permissive parenting is lackadaisical or hands-off and has been associated with delayed maturity in children.[37]

What can you do to raise a happier child to become a happier adult? Reward and praise are important to bolster self-esteem, confidence and willingness to take on more challenging roles, but they need to be calibrated to success. If you overly praise your child, you will make them happy initially because this is what they require from loving adults, but the danger is that you will unwittingly undermine their mastery. When every outcome becomes a 'good job' by default, your child will not learn to discriminate between success and failure. Over time, this will make them less independent and resilient when you are not around. Take an active interest in your child's efforts, supporting them where you can with encouragement and advice, but do not lavish them with unwarranted praise. Rather, step back and allow them to make their own mistakes to learn from in a non-judgmental way, so that there is no pressure for them to succeed in order to gain your unconditional love. Give them guidance, allow them to flourish but neither ignore nor stifle them. Provide the parental scaffold to support them rather than constrain them.

We began this lesson with the finding that happy kids tend to grow up into happy adults. That happiness as a child is largely due to their supporting relationships with others, but what determines the ability to form healthy relationships? There are a number of mechanisms, but emotional regulation – the ability to manage our emotions – is a big factor. We control ourselves through activity of the *prefrontal cortical* regions of the brain (the outer layers towards the front), which take the longest to develop and play a major role in coordinating the various systems that generate our minds.

Prefrontal systems do not reach maturity until adulthood, which partly explains why adolescents can be impulsive and experience disorganised thoughts and behaviours. In pre-schoolers these systems fail to regulate the emotional outbursts and temper tantrums that are observed at this age. Lack of impulse control also explains the egocentric thinking of children who cannot suppress their own perspective on the Piagetian Three Mountains task, or the theory of mind tasks we encountered earlier, because they can't suppress the urge to say what they know to be true. They can't stop themselves saying 'pencils' when they really should be answering 'Smarties'.[38] Even adults can experience impulsive and disorganised thoughts when their prefrontal systems are not working properly. One of the effects of alcohol is to impair prefrontal functions, which is why inebriated adults become disinhibited. Emotional regulation is important for anger management – to keep a cool head when tempers are rising.[39] One benefit of slow maturing prefrontal systems is that we can adapt and modify our behaviour to a multitude of different social norms, rules and cultures that are constantly changing. Neuroscientist Sarah-Jayne Blakemore argues that through the extended development of the prefrontal systems, we 'invent ourselves' by establishing the regulatory networks necessary to operate as adults.[40]

As mature adults we depend on the control provided by the

prefrontal cortical systems. With age, they increasingly perform so-called *executive functions*, including planning and reasoning, as well as suppressing irrelevant or intrusive thoughts. Stability, consistency and regularity during childhood enable the maturing brain to encode adaptive ways of behaving because these parameters enable children to detect and recognise patterns and anticipate how to respond. This provides mastery over the situation 'If I do this, then they are likely to do that.' This ability to predict, facilitated by a theory of mind, enables us to navigate the complex social worlds we inhabit.

The looking-glass self

The final sense of self that is relevant to our happiness is the way we think others think about us. Who we are is dependent on others' opinions. We may believe we are the funniest joker in the world, but if no one else is laughing, are we really funny? This is what sociologist Charles Cooley calls the 'looking-glass self' – the notion that the self is a reflection of what others think about us.[41] The problem is that we can't really know what others truly think about us. We can only imagine how we are perceived, which creates a formula for a constantly shifting self, captured by Cooley's conundrum 'I am not what I think I am, and I am not what you think I am; I am what I think that you think I am.'

The looking-glass self is why we often feel we are not being true to our self. We behave differently in the boardroom, the bedroom, on the playing field or among the different groups we are members of, and this makes us uncomfortable. Being consistent within each of these relationships is desirable so that we maintain integrity, but you can't behave the same way across different groups because that would be inappropriate. You can be romantic with a lover but must remain professional with a colleague. Expressing insecurities and vulnerabilities may be regarded as appropriate in one situation (e.g. therapy) but not others (e.g. job interviews). Sometimes this can feel like being a different person. In these moments we can feel a loss of identity. The current controversy surrounding identity politics reflects the tensions that exist between how individuals regard themselves and how society regards them. Some of us believe that we have never had the opportunity to be our true self. Maybe this is why the number-one regret among terminally ill patients is that they didn't have the courage to live a life true to their authentic self rather than the life others expected of them.[42]

When we are unhappy, we beat ourselves up over our failures and our bad decisions and choices. We attribute these failings to our self. But we do not choose the environments we are raised in, nor can we control all the experiences that come to influence us. Our autobiographies are ghost-written by others. Once we appreciate that the self is constructed from a multitude of factors, we can start to lift that burden from our shoulders. If we can step back so that we are less emotionally invested, we can find a healthier perspective. This is what I mean by becoming less egocentric and more allocentric.

Becoming less egocentric triggers a psychological process known as *detachment* or *decentering*. Detachment is not indifference or a denial of thoughts and emotions. Rather, it is the act of viewing these mental states objectively, which is a more productive way of introducing a psychological distance between yourself and your mental experiences. In Lesson Five,

I'll explain why detachment works as a technique to combat intrusive negative thoughts.

In the meantime, here is a happiness hack for detaching yourself from upsetting emotions and thoughts.

If you get upset, say out loud, 'I am not my feelings, my emotions, my past or my beliefs.' Rather, say, 'I am someone who has feelings, beliefs and emotions.' You can say, 'I am not an anxious person. No, I am a person having an anxious thought.'

This subtle shift in language changes our self-perception from someone who is and will always be anxious into someone who is currently experiencing a temporary bout of anxiety that will pass. This is a much more positive and optimistic way of thinking that we revisit in Lesson Four.

Some people believe that getting rid of the self is the answer to becoming happier. Buddhism advocates *annatta* or 'no self' as the goal to enlightened happiness, achieved by letting go of all the components that generate the experience of self. We will describe in later lessons how meditation, rituals and psychedelics that radically alter our perception of self can be therapeutic for healthier mental lives, but they are not for everyone. Sometimes such practices lead to *depersonalisation*. Symptoms of depersonalisation include feelings that you're an outside observer of your thoughts, feelings, your body or parts of your body – as if you were floating in air above yourself or feeling like a robot, or that you're not in control of your speech or movements. Feeling a loss of control appears to be a critical factor underlying the negative experience following depersonalisation. However, if we can take control over our egocentric self and voluntarily project our thoughts and behaviours to be more allocentric, then that will generate a positive experience that underpins our path to becoming happier.

The integrated sense of self must have evolved for the betterment of our species. It's there for a good reason, as a way of keeping track of conscious experiences, of organising thoughts and interacting with others. We don't need to annihilate our self for a healthier mind, but we can dampen down or quieten the egocentric self to allow others to be heard. We can gain some distance from the I-self when we are ruminating on the negative. We can learn to appreciate that we operate with multiple versions of our self that mirror the expectations and opinions of others, but also that we must not become too overly dependent on what others think – because if we become overly compliant, others become aware of our duplicity, which leads them to question the reliability of their models of us. We in turn become aware that we are in constant flux trying to please others. Achieving balance between the egocentric and allocentric self is key to our pursuit of happiness. The self is not cast in stone, and that is a liberating thought. We can alter our ego.

Happiness exercises

Start a journal. Invest in a good-quality notebook and pens. Paper is better than digital. Update your journal as regularly as possible. Journaling puts things into perspective and provides a record of your life and how it changes.

Dig out any old diaries and letters that you have kept. Not only does this remind us of how our self has changed, but these records prove that we overcome most of the problems and concerns that we used to worry about.

Adopt an allocentric perspective the next time you have conflict. Try to take another's perspective on situations. Rather than saying, 'You do not understand', try instead, 'I am not making myself clear.' This should lessen the negative feelings but is also more likely to lead to resolution.

Support and encourage your child, but do not dominate or overly praise their efforts. Be positive and focus on the successes but do not go overboard. Otherwise, they will get used to the praise and come to expect it even when it is unwarranted.

Detach yourself from upsetting emotions and thoughts by saying out loud, 'I am not my feelings, my emotions, my past or beliefs.' Rather, say, 'I am someone who has feelings, beliefs and emotions.' This subtle switch in language alters the ego.

LESSON TWO

Avoid Isolation

Very few of us could last long in the wild without the skills and knowledge of how to live off the land. Left to our own devices, most of us would starve. We have become dependent on technology, civilisation and the conveniences of the modern world, but even with all of these comforts, we still require something more basic: the company of others – not only for our survival but for our emotional well-being. Our happiness depends on others. Why did humans become so socially dependent? The answer is a lot less obvious than you think. It has to do with brains, giving birth and raising children.

Every species has a *life-history strategy*.[1] These are evolved patterns that describe the way animals live, their reproduction and their lifespan. Some animals live short lives, others live longer. Some live in relative isolation and others live in large groups. Some have one offspring that they protect and nurture, others have numerous progeny that they abandon to face the elements by themselves. Some mate for life, others are promiscuous. All of these patterns have evolved to optimise the survival of each species under constantly changing conditions.

While humans may live long or short lives as individuals, be hermits or socialites, have many or no children, prefer to mate for life or never, we are still a species that has an overall life-history strategy. That life-history strategy has been shaped primarily by the evolution of the human brain – a brain that enabled prosociality but also depended on it. The evolution of the brain also explains why we have emotions like happiness and why some of the greatest joys are derived from our interactions with others.

In comparison to other primates, our life-history strategy is characterised by relatively long lives, more offspring and survival beyond the age of reproduction.[2] We also tend to form strong and long relationships and we spend much of our energy and attention focused on our loved ones. This forges the relationship between early social interactions and later happiness as positive social interactions are consistently the strongest predictors of an individual's happiness. For example, in the longest study of well-being, conducted on Boston men for eighty years from 1934 and known as the Harvard Study of Adult Development, the most consistent predictor of happiness was good social relationships.[3]

Humans have the longest childhoods in the animal kingdom because we also have proportionally the biggest brain. The brain is about seven times larger than it should be, given our average body size. Brains are metabolically hungry so there must have been a good reason to evolve this expensive adaptation and allow it to keep expanding. One intriguing explanation has become known as the *social brain hypothesis*.[4]

Avoid Isolation

According to the psychologist Robin Dunbar, who popularised the concept, if you look across the animal kingdom, those mammals who live in the more complex social groups have larger brains. Dunbar argues that complex social arrangements are particularly challenging, but with bigger brains, you can keep track of more pieces of information to successfully navigate the social landscape. One study was able to demonstrate that brain size in humans predicted the extent of social networks depending on the individual's capacity for applying theory of mind.[5] Big brains enable us to predict what others are thinking and what they'll do next.

Human intelligence increased because we lived in complex groups, developed the language capacity to share information and learned to cooperate.[6] This created a positive feedback loop known as *cultural ratcheting*, where knowledge acquired in one generation was passed on to the next, thereby accumulating more expertise and wisdom over time.[7] The human capacity for living and learning together explains why our species has evolved so rapidly over the past 200,000 years.

In order to grow our large brains, however, we had to extend the period of early development and prioritise the precious energy allocation to the brain. This explains why young children's heads are so big relative to their bodies: most energy resources are being diverted to the brain during the early years. The newborn brain weighs about 350 grams – a quarter of the adult brain, at 1.5kg or about 3lbs. It represents 10 per cent of the infant's body weight, whereas the adult brain is about 2 per cent of the total body. Most of this difference is made up within the first six to seven years, by which time the child's brain has tripled in size. Later, as brain energy requirements subside, our bodies start to accelerate in growth with the re-allocation of energy.

Big-brained children, however, present a considerable problem for mothers. When our ancient ancestors came down from the trees and began to walk upright, this changed the anatomy of the human body. Moving efficiently on two legs requires narrow hips, otherwise you would waddle as chimpanzees do when they try to walk upright. To outrun predators and capture prey, there was adaptive pressure to keep human hips from becoming too wide, which in turn meant that the pelvic cavity, the space in between the hips, could not become any larger. In females, the pelvic cavity determines the size of the birth canal, which determines the size of the baby's head that a mother can deliver. The problem is that with our evolving social brain, it increased to be three to four times larger than the brain of our ancestral apes, which made hominid childbirth more difficult. Even with a skull that is relatively soft and ends up squeezed into the shape of a sugarloaf during delivery, giving birth has been likened to passing a 'watermelon or a bowling ball' through a 'ring of fire'.[8]

There are some mothers who give birth effortlessly, and a few who give birth alone, but they are both the minority. Most human births are difficult, painful and require physical assistance or midwifery. This is not the case for our wide-hipped cousins the chimpanzees, who go off by themselves and usually deliver in a couple of hours without all the commotion and pain.[9] Midwifery is extremely rare in non-human primates but a stable and universal feature of human behaviour. When you consider the time, the effort, the pain and possibility of opportunist predators, human childbirth was only viable through the assistance from others – but who were these early birthing partners and why did they bother to help?

It is likely that the first midwives were the mother's mother (the child's grandmother) and the aunts who are most genetically related. Mothers who lived long enough to assist in the delivery of their own daughter's children would have conferred an advantage for living beyond the age of reproduction because their offspring would carry the genes for longevity. This *grandmother hypothesis* explains the evolutionary value of female humans who live on well past the menopause – the age beyond which they cannot bear children.[10] Mathematical modelling of human evolution shows that the appearance of grandmothers increased human life expectancy.[11] The childrearing assistance provided by grandmothers would have enabled the human lifespan to double from twenty-five years to fifty in less than 60,000 years, thereby increasing the opportunity for cultural ratcheting and for wisdom to be passed on. Remember this the next time you're irritated by the old lady in the queue in front of you as she struggles to remember her PIN number. Your longer life expectancy and intelligence is down to your ancestral grandmothers.

After giving birth, mother and baby would have also benefitted from the help of others, not just those who were most genetically related. The African proverb that it takes a village to raise a child is true not only with regards to the practicalities of looking after our young but also to the way children are shaped by the group. As noted in the last lesson, we are emotionally invested in young children and such compassion could have emerged as a stable human trait that fostered social connectedness within the group.[12] In this way, the demands of raising children shaped human society. Parents who needed help in childrearing would be expected to reciprocate with the birth of others in the tribe. These cooperative individuals would have reproduced more successfully and passed on traits such as compassion to their offspring, thus increasing the likelihood of prosocial behaviour becoming an established pattern in the species. If you add emotional rewards such as joy and happiness into the childrearing mix, then you have a powerful combination for spreading and establishing social connectedness.

It's not just the challenge of raising children that requires emotional bonds within the group. The social brain hypothesis predicts that animals living in large social groups will also form alliances among non-related individuals to achieve goals and avoid individual conflicts. In humans, we call these alliances friendships, which generate and are held together by varying degrees of positive emotions. Dunbar examines how and why friendships form, how they are maintained and why they sometimes break down. He identifies circles of friendship from 'just friends, good friends, best friends, close friends, to intimate friends', with each level providing different levels of emotional support and commitment. All of them generate and require positive emotional engagement. Through these interactions, we evolved into the species we are today – one that coexists, cooperates and requires social sustenance and emotional attachment to survive.[13]

Emotional attachment

If you have ever watched ducklings relentlessly following their mother around, it's clear to see that the ducklings have a biological drive to maintain close proximity. If a distance opens up, the ducklings chirp more loudly to signal to the mother that she needs to return to her brood. Humans are no different. If you watch a young toddler with their mother, there appears to be an invisible elastic band connecting them. Nothing is more arresting than the wail of a distressed child; a baby's cry is a biological siren that triggers a strong negative emotional reaction in adults to respond.[14] Some children are more independent and there are cultural and individual differences in how comfortable parents are in being separated from their children, but it is human nature to form strong emotional bonds or attachment to our young.[15]

British psychiatrist John Bowlby argued that this primeval emotional bond was necessary to ensure survival and that anything that disrupted attachment was detrimental to the normal course of development.[16] He came to this conclusion based on his studies of children whose home lives had been disrupted by separation from their families when they were evacuated from London during the bombing raids of the Second World War. Bowlby discovered that many evacuees went on to develop behavioural problems and argued that children need not only food and comfort but emotional attachment or love from an early age.

Attachment research is one of the major areas of developmental psychology because we all have opinions on how our parents affected our development and many of us are concerned with how best to raise our own children. Psychology has a history of offering parental advice that has not always been good, such as physical punishment ('If you spare the rod, you'll spoil the child!'), but Bowlby's general idea about the importance of early social environments has stood the test of time. Research on development across the animal kingdom using behavioural and neuroscience techniques has shown that there is a drive to form a strong emotional connection with others from birth, known as *secure attachment*, especially in those animals that live in social groups.

In the 1950s and '60s, the psychologist Harry Harlow would go on to test Bowlby's claims by raising rhesus infant monkeys in isolation.[17] Even though they were provided with all the necessities, like food and warmth, for survival, socially isolated individuals developed severe behavioural problems and found it difficult to reintegrate when they were introduced back to other monkeys. They would not mate when they reached maturity, and those females who were artificially inseminated were incapable of raising their offspring as mothers. They ignored, rejected and sometimes killed their own babies. What's significant is that the effects of social isolation were most damaging during the first six months of life. If infant rhesus monkeys spent only three months in isolation, they could recover. If they were isolated *after* six months, they were also relatively unimpaired. It was the monkeys who spent all of their first six months in isolation who were the most negatively impaired. This indicates that in rhesus monkeys, to whom humans are distantly related, the first six months represent a critical period for attachment and subsequent normal social behaviour.

Harlow would later establish that the effects of early

deprivation could be reversed after six months by pairing the isolated individuals with normally reared young 'therapist' monkeys who were intent on forming a relationship.[18] Even though the therapist monkeys were initially rebuffed by the isolated monkeys, after a few weeks of persistent play, the isolated monkeys began to show signs of normal social behaviour and by the end of the first year they were fully recovered. This indicates that rehabilitation after extreme social deprivation is possible, but it requires social integration.

Though it's unethical to test Bowlby's theory on human children, support for the critical period for attachment and the long-term effects of early social isolation on human development have been found in orphans raised in appalling conditions of depravity. In 1990, following the collapse of the Romanian communist dictatorship under Nicolae Ceaușescu, state-run institutions were full of children who had been abandoned by their parents. Ceaușescu had pressurised women to have at least five babies, and if they used contraception or had an abortion, mothers faced the possibility of imprisonment. As a result, when the economy crashed, impoverished parents were forced to abandon the children that they could no longer look after.

On arriving at the orphanages, rescuers found conditions that were the worst they had had ever seen. Young children were chained to beds and left in their own excrement, then hosed down with cold water when the smell became too overwhelming. There was little or no social interaction with carers, who had on average over thirty children each to look after. There was no love or attachment here. Hundreds of orphans were rescued – taken in and raised by foster families in countries including the USA, the UK, Canada and the Netherlands. How would they fare in a new home?

Thirty years on, these orphans are now fully-grown adults living in the West. Initially, on leaving the orphanages, the children were malnourished and scored low on behavioural measures of intelligence, but they recovered quickly, with few signs of long-term problems – except for those who had spent longer than the first six months of their lives in the orphanage.[19] Over the years, some of these individuals exhibited behavioural problems at schools and experienced emotional difficulties as young adults. Growing up, these individuals were described as having 'quasi-autism' because they exhibited some of the characteristic social withdrawal symptoms associated with autism.[20] Something in their brain had gone very wrong during those first critical six months – the same period as for Harlow's rhesus monkeys.[21]

Without secure attachment to a primary caregiver from the very beginning, children develop so-called *disinhibited attachment*. Behaviourally, as they age, children exhibiting disinhibited attachment do not seek out a particular adult or differentiate between adults. They readily wander off with strangers and there is a lack of checking back with the parent in anxiety-provoking situations. Disinhibited children are indiscriminate in their friendships and find it difficult to form close, confiding relationships with others. This social inadequacy had knock-on effects for the vulnerable Romanian orphans. Although there was full recovery of cognitive skills, with intelligence relatively unaffected by this harsh start in life, there were long-term negative consequences from social isolation on their emotional lives, despite all of the subsequent nurturing care and love provided by the adoptive families.[22]

Social integration remains a critical component of normal development and, later, adult well-being. Like most aspects of human behaviour, social skills vary on a continuum, but we all require the company of others because this is how we evolved. It is the primary source of our happiness, which is why being ignored, excluded or even rejected can be so upsetting.

Social death

As we noted in Lesson One, happy kids tend to grow up into happy adults. Being accepted by others is critically important to being a happy child, but the playground is fraught with allegiances and politics that require astute social intelligence to navigate. From a very early age, pre-school children use peer exclusion to manipulate relationships – with girls using this strategy twice as much as boys.[23]

Social aggression is the term used to describe the non-physical harm that individuals can inflict upon others by exclusion, rumourmongering and basically anything that undermines the social status of others. One form of social aggression, known as *ostracism* – being ignored or excluded – is particularly hurtful and problematic among teenagers. A study of social aggression in over 4,800 children aged nine to thirteen found that they would prefer to experience physical violence rather than be excluded.[24] Even as adults we experience the pain of isolation. In his autobiography, describing his time as a political prisoner on Robben Island, Nelson Mandela wrote, 'Nothing is more dehumanizing than the absence of human companionship' and that he knew men in prison who preferred half a dozen lashes with a whip to being in solitary confinement.[25] Feeling alone is one of the worst feelings in the world.

The fear of ostracism remains a primary concern throughout life. It is a common occurrence, with one study reporting that most people are ignored or excluded at least once a day on average,[26] but ostracism never really loses its impact. It is so powerful that we are automatically sensitive to any indication that we are being excluded. The psychologist Kip Williams discovered this by chance during a memorable encounter as he sat with his dog on the campus park of Purdue University, Indiana, where he worked. On that day, a frisbee hit him on the back. He turned around to see two guys playing and so he flicked it skilfully back to the pair, who then began tossing the frisbee to Williams. He was pleased to have struck up a spontaneous game with a couple of strangers, but after about four minutes the others stopped throwing to Williams. Imagine how awkward that must have been, standing there waiting for the frisbee. Do you wait for the return throw or just slink off? Williams felt the immediate negative emotional impact of ostracism.

After reflecting on his own emotional reaction to the rejection, Williams set out to study how sensitive we are to being excluded. He developed an online game known as Cyberball to simulate his frisbee encounter where participants virtually tossed a ball back and forth between themselves and two simulated players.[27] And just like his experience in the park, after a minute or so the computer arranged that the ball was not passed back to the human participant but only between the two other players. How would people respond to this computerised ostracism?

Remarkably, even though it is just a simple computer game, ostracism by Cyberball is very powerful. A large-scale analysis of 120 studies that have used the paradigm on over 11,000 players (a meta-analysis) reveals that the induced ostracism produces very large and very robust negative effects.[28] Participants reported a negative mood, lower self-esteem and a loss of control after being ostracised, even though they knew they were not playing with other people and that the program was rigged. Our reaction to ostracism is like a reflex wired into us through evolution.

Social isolation, ostracism, exclusion and rejection all have immediate and long-term negative consequences for mental well-being. Williams calls exclusion 'the kiss of social death'.[29] He went on to identify three stages of reaction to ostracism, comprising a) reflexive social pain that is immediate and automatic, b) a reflective stage where the individual tries to rationalise and cope with the situation, and finally c) a resignation stage that occurs after prolonged ostracism.

Becoming isolated make us unhappy but therein lies the explanation for why we have these negative emotional reactions. It is a negative punishment that motivates us to avoid exclusion. Just like physical pain, the social pain of isolation is a warning to change. Indeed, the very same areas in the brain activated by physical pain are also triggered by the pain of social loss.[30] This pain triggers a set of coping mechanisms to reinstate ourselves back into the social group that threatens to expel us. As soon as it becomes clear that we are in danger of being ostracised, we become hyper-alert and vigilant, looking for opportunities to ingratiate ourselves with others. If these reinstatement strategies fail, this leads to helplessness, alienation, depression and feelings of unworthiness. Eventually, isolation can lead to an earlier death.

Loneliness: the solitary killer

Psychologist Julianne Holt-Lunstad used to put people under pressure for a living. Interested in how stress affects blood pressure, she would invite participants into her lab and get them to do a bit of public speaking – the number-one thing most people find anxiety-inducing. What she found was that very often, those participants who were accompanied by supportive friends reacted much better to her tests compared with those who turned up alone.[31] Even something as tangible as physical pain can be tolerated more when we are accompanied by a loved one. In one Scandinavian study, participants had pressure applied to their index fingernails to measure their tolerance to pain, either when they were alone or accompanied by a romantic partner. When the loved one was present, the heroic participants could tolerate significantly more pressure applied to their sensitive fingernails and reported less pain compared than individuals who were 'tortured' alone.[32]

If our reactions to pain can be influenced by the presence of others, what about the role of others in our lives when it comes to longer-term outcomes? Do others make a difference to our lifespan? To answer this, Holt-Lunstad analysed studies from across the world to look at whether social connectedness impacted on health in later years. What she found was that individuals who were more socially connected were 50 per cent more likely to be alive at the end of the study compared with the group who were the least socially connected.[33] In fact, when she looked at the various well-known factors that contribute to life expectancy – such as genetic disposition, availability of quality medical intervention and healthy life-styles such as exercise and dieting – she found that they pale in comparison to the strongest predictor: social connectedness.

Loneliness may make us unhappy, but it can also kill. In 2023, the journal *American Surgeon* issued a report[34] on an epidemic of loneliness and isolation in the US, where 50 per cent of the population report poor social connection.[35] The report estimates that 'the physical health consequences of poor or insufficient connection include a 29 per cent increased risk of heart disease, a 32 per cent increased risk of stroke, and a 50 per cent increased risk of developing dementia for older adults'. In terms of threat to life, it has been estimated that social isolation and loneliness represent a greater risk factor for an earlier death than other well-known unhealthy factors such as obesity and the smoking of fifteen cigarettes a day.[36] What could possibly explain this relationship between loneliness and life expectancy? How can the lonely mind affect the body? The answer comes down to how we react to stress and to the support we receive from others.

Stress

When threatened, humans engage a rapid physiological system that has become known as the 'fight or flight' response, which refers to the strategies of either confrontation or running away. It should be called the 'fight, flight or freeze' response as many animals, including humans sometimes, become involuntarily immobile when faced with danger, which is why we talk of 'paralysing fear'. It is the body's response to challenges that triggers increased blood pressure, heart rate, breathing, sweating and other physiological changes – such as the widening of the pupils of your eyes to see more clearly in the dark – which prepare you for threats. This response is the *sympathetic* part of the autonomic nervous system, which, as the name autonomous suggests, is a relatively automatic system that is not under voluntary control. In short bursts, these sympathetic changes are adaptive, mobilising and energising the body quickly to deal with potential threats.

One problem with fight-or-flight, however, is that very often, when the danger has passed or turns out to be a false alarm, we can't easily return to feeling relaxed. Individuals who suffer from anxiety, the most common form of mental health issue, have an overactive fight-or-flight response. Some fears are specific, as in the case of phobias, but more often than not, anxiety is generalised anxiety – a state of being in constant fear in the absence of any obvious danger. This is the most common type of anxiety disorder. Occasionally there may be acute episodes of panic attacks, associated with hyperventilating and overwhelming thoughts of dread. After generalised anxiety, social anxiety, or social phobia, is the next most commonly reported problem, which is why public speaking is stressful. As the name suggests, social anxiety arises in situations where one experiences anxiety in the company of others. Extreme social anxiety can be debilitating, as it can make people isolate and withdraw, but this may compound the problem of isolation. For example, in a 1998 study, adolescents with social phobia were found to be more likely to have avoided social interactions as younger children.[37] Avoiding any social interaction becomes a self-fulfilling prophecy, with the risk of losing the benefits of engaging with others.

When anxiety from stress becomes chronic, it can produce long-term health problems. Chronic stress impacts on the *hypothalamic-pituitary-adrenocortical* (HPA) axis – a system that coordinates the body's release of hormones, especially cortisol.[38] One critical function of the HPA is to eventually counter the effects of the fight-flight and return the body to a resting state in preparation for the next threat. However, if the HPA remains activated because the threat is still perceived, even when it is absent, then this has long-term consequences for future reactivity. The HPA becomes deregulated and loses its ability to respond appropriately because either there is too much, or too little, reactivity. This means that levels of cortisol fluctuate between extremely high to extremely low levels, producing unstable and erratic states that can impact on the body's immune system – including the *T-lymphocytes* or so-called 'killer cells' that fight disease. When the immune system is impaired or dysfunctional, life expectancy is shortened.

Early experiences of being raised in stressful environments imprints onto a child's HPA response, creating a dysfunctional system that is ill-prepared to deal with future stress.[39] Maternal stress can also be passed on to the unborn children. For example, mothers who witnessed the 9/11 terrorist attack on New York's World Trade Center when pregnant and then went on to develop post-traumatic stress disorder as a result were found to have lower resting cortisol levels, indicative of a dysfunctional HPA response.[40] This abnormality was also observed in their infants, who were foetuses in the third trimester of pregnancy, when the developing immune system is most sensitive. In this way early stressful experiences get under our skin.

Stress also interferes with decision-making. In his book *Thinking, Fast and Slow*, the Nobel Prize-winning psychologist Daniel Kahneman draws a distinction between the emotional–intuitive System One versus the rational–analytic System Two.[41] System One is fast and furious, whereas System Two is slow and cool-headed. Think Captain Kirk versus Mr Spock. Stress shifts people towards the more rapid, impulsive thinking of System One, where we feel the pressure to act immediately; when threatened, people respond more emotionally, from the perspective of System One.[42] A racing mind is one that is prone to speeding to the wrong conclusions, and if this mode of thinking dominates, then this leads to chronic anxiety.

When we are in fight-flight mode, we are likely to interpret situations as more threatening than they really are. We experience the rush of the hormone *adrenaline* when tempers rise, leading to overreaction and confrontation. Road rage provides a good example. According to the American Automobile Association (AAA), eight out of ten drivers admitted to aggressive driving (e.g. tailgating, switching lanes to block another driver), with males being more aggressive than females.[43] Over a third (35 per cent) of US males and a quarter of females (28 per cent) say they flipped the finger or honked at another driver in 2020. The AAA attributes this aggressive behaviour to stress and frustration. In the cold light of day, road rage that has ended in violent altercation seems ridiculous, but these incidents arise because the same anger that saved us in the past, when confronted by real enemies, is not calibrated to deal with the lesser irritations that arise from living in the modern world. We are too quick to overreact, and once unleashed, rage is difficult to rein in with reason.

If you are someone who gets angry or anxious (and we all do), then there is a simple way to shut down the fight-flight response. One technique is 'box breathing', which is used by US Navy SEALs. To do this, visualise the geometric outline of a square in your mind and start at the bottom left corner. Begin by breathing in through your nostrils for a count of four seconds: *'In*–2, 3, 4' – as you do so, move your attention up, breathing in slowly for the count of four until you reach the top left corner. Notice how your chest rises. Next is *'Hold*–2, 3, 4' – as you hold your breath, move your attention across the top line for the count of four until you reach the top right-hand corner. Then *'Out*–2, 3, 4' while letting your breath out through your mouth, moving your attention downwards to the bottom right corner. Notice how your chest falls. When you reach the bottom corner, complete the square with *'Wait*–2, 3, 4', resting and not breathing as you move back along the bottom line to the starting corner to begin the box circuit again.

This technique helps you to control your breathing. It activates the second part of the autonomic nervous system, known as the *parasympathetic* response, which counteracts the sympathetic activity of the fight-flight response. This 'rest and digest' response slows the heart rate into a regular rhythm, decreases blood pressure and relaxes the muscles. The combination of controlled breathing, monitoring your chest movements, visualisation of the square and shifting attention works by directing your focus away from whatever is triggering the fight-flight response. Once the sympathetic response is under control, you can address the stress using System Two reasoning to rationalise the situation.

Stress is a well-recognised contributing factor to disease, and there is abundant evidence that social connection reduces stress. The mechanisms by which social connection reduces stress operate in a number of ways. First, people who feel connected are motivated to engage in greater self-regulatory behaviour, such as looking after themselves and using preventive health-care services.[44] Friends and loved ones can encourage us to lead healthier lives by losing weight, exercising, getting more sleep and taking medications. For example, adolescents are far more likely to be physically active if their friends are.[45] Finally, when we feel connected to others, we do not feel isolated and vulnerable, so our perception of threats are reduced, making them more tolerable. We can even talk problems over and get a better sense of perspective with a little help from our friends.

Helping others

Throughout this lesson I have argued that as social animals we thrive in groups and languish in isolation. I recommend that the path to happiness is best pursued by becoming less egocentric and more other-focused. One way to do that is to be generous. Despite a challenging global pandemic when finances were tight, more than half the British public donated £11.3 billion to charity in 2020, up 10 per cent from the year before.[46] There was a similar pattern in the US, where 2020 broke the record for charitable giving with an estimated $471 billion.[47] Even at a time when it would be in our best interests to be selfish, many showed themselves to be altruistic. Why?

Other animals usually help each other when they are genetically related[48] or the help is reciprocated.[49] Both reasons, known as 'kin selection' and 'reciprocal altruism' respectively, are evolved strategies for the survival of the genes we inherit. Kin selection makes sense from an evolutionary point of view: even though helping others may come at a cost or disadvantage to oneself, if you are related to the person you are helping, then you both share a proportion of the same genes, including those that incline you to help, so you are providing benefit to the survival of those mutual strings of biological code.

Reciprocal altruism is when we help others we are not related to. At first, reciprocal altruism seems more difficult to understand as there is no obvious genetic benefit. One bizarre example of reciprocal altruism comes from the blood-sucking vampire bat of South America. If, after a night's hunting, a particular bat has been unsuccessful, other bats will regurgitate some of the blood they have swallowed to feed their hungry nestmate – but only if they can be trusted to return the favour.[50] Bats who have reneged on such blood pacts in the past gain a reputation for being selfish and are ignored in the future, should they go hungry. Given the unpredictability of meals, reciprocal altruism is a strategy to get individuals through lean times. If you have a particularly good day hunting, then sharing with others less successful creates a debt to be paid back when you are not so fortunate.

Human-helping behaviour also operates as kin selection and reciprocal altruism would predict, but where we seem to differ from other animals is our willingness to help when there is no family connection nor an expectation to get anything in return. At first glance, this may seem to make no sense from an evolutionary point of view, but in fact it does. Being kind not only benefits others, but it helps us too. Generosity can signal virtue, which increases our reputation. This is a phenomenon observed in many different cultures to raise the social status of the individual. For example, charitable online donations are influenced by the visibility of what peers have previously donated, especially among males when the fundraiser is an attractive female.[51] The higher the average donation, the more subsequent donors give. Through signalling we can demonstrate that we are kind and caring – attributes that can raise our social standing. When it comes to altruistic acts, individuals effectively compete to be seen to be more generous.

Virtue signalling may explain some acts of altruism, but it can't explain anonymous donations. When handed a sum of money with no strings attached, 60 per cent of individuals still give around one fifth to an anonymous recipient when asked to make a donation.[52] What's going on here? Part of the answer comes down to normative behaviour. Even in anonymous situations, we tend to conform with what we think others would do in the same situation. When we find ourselves in a situation where a charitable donation is implied, we tend to comply because we think that is what is expected of us, but less so when we are told that it is okay to take money from someone else.[53]

With all of these alternative explanations for acts of kindness, is there any milk of human goodness left? Are we ever truly altruistic? It's an interesting moral question. There's even an episode of the hit sitcom *Friends* that addresses the issue, when Joey describes Phoebe's willingness to become her brother's surrogate mother to his babies as a selfish act because Phoebe feels good about helping her kin.[54] Joey says, 'Well, it made *you* feel good, so that makes it selfish,' and then challenges her to come up with a truly selfless act that does not involve feeling good about oneself. Phoebe is dumbstruck because even the most selfless act could be described as selfish if it makes you feel good. The rest of the episode then focuses on Phoebe's attempts to disprove Joey and find examples of selfless acts, to comic effect.

Unconditional kindness seems the most selfless of acts but in fact it is a way to boost our own happiness. For example, those of us who are not normally generous might assume it is better to spend money on ourselves rather than spend it on others. We might turn to retail therapy to make ourselves feel better, but this strategy is misguided. In one of the most famous positive psychology studies,[55] Elizabeth Dunn and her colleagues gave individuals envelopes containing either $5 or $20, with the instructions either that by the end of the day they were to spend the money either on themselves or on another individual. When assessed on measures of happiness, and contrary to the prediction that we will be happier spending the money on ourselves, those who spent the money on a stranger, such as buying them a cup of coffee when waiting in the Starbucks queue, felt much happier. The amount didn't matter; rather, it was the act of giving that produced the feeling of happiness. This is what economists call the 'warm glow' of giving – a feelgood factor in the knowledge that we have helped others.[56] This link between unconditional generosity and personal happiness has been found in a study of 200,000 people across 136 countries.[57] Even in poor countries such as Uganda, where $5 is a considerable amount to give away, the same happiness boost has been observed when people are instructed to spend money on others.

Abraham Lincoln once said, 'When I do good, I feel good. When I do bad, I feel bad. That's my religion.' There is something intrinsically rewarding about acts of kindness. Being good feels good. Generosity activates two areas of the brain.[58] The first area, deep in the brain just behind your ears, known as the *ventral striatum*, is the so-called reward centre, where the feel-good factor is generated. The second area, the *temporal parietal junction*, further up and towards the back of your head, is one region where we identify other people. As the generosity increases, so does the activity between these two areas, as well as the self-reports of happiness. In our brains, we hold representations (patterns of neural activity) for ourselves and separate representations of others. When you help others, you are increasing your brain's representation of your self-concept as connected with others and then reinforcing this association with emotional reward. In effect, when you help others, you are rewarding yourself with happiness. By this logic, you might agree with Joey from *Friends* and argue that there can never be a truly selfless act. But if both parties benefit, what's the harm?

If you do want to boost your happiness, try a little act of unconditional kindness. It is best when the kindness is spontaneous and anonymous. Otherwise, we tend to rationalise it and it loses its impact on our happiness. In one study,[59] recipients were given one card from two sets, all with a $1 coin taped to them and the message: 'This is for you! [From] The Smile Society, A Student/Community Secular Alliance. We like to promote Random Acts of Kindness! Have a nice day!' One set had the same information but also included the questions 'Who are we?' and 'Why we do this?' that provided an explanatory context as to why the money was being given away.

People who received the card with the explanations were less curious and less happy twenty minutes later than people who received the card on the left. When the gift was unexpected and unexplained, this had a greater positive impact on happiness. So, if you want to generate the most happiness that gives you the warmest glow, perform unconditional acts of kindness with a little bit of mystery thrown in – but expect nothing in return.

Too much social media is making children unhappy

If growing happier can be achieved by reaching out and being kind to others, then we should be in a modern era of expanding happiness through the newfound opportunities provided by digital technologies. Never in the history of human civilisation have individuals had the opportunity to connect with so many other people. Anyone with a smartphone can broadcast to the world relatively cheaply and effortlessly. Social media offers continuous interaction regardless of time of day or geographic location, opening up limitless opportunities for becoming more allocentric.

And yet, since its arrival, social media has become the scourge of mental well-being, with critics decrying its negative impact on society. It seems to have taken over human activity. Social media is designed to capture our attention by tapping into our deep-seated need to be recognised, connected and validated by others – even when we are with our friends. It mainlines directly into our egocentric self. In many ways, the appropriate abbreviation for social media should be *So... Me*. It takes a strong- willed individual to turn off their phones or ignore notifications. One survey in January 2024 estimated that 62 per cent of the world's population uses social media, with an average daily usage of two hours and thirty- three minutes.[60] More than one in three internet minutes can be attributed to social media platforms. And that's just the average!

Whenever a new transformative technology emerges and is widely adopted by the general public, a phenomenon known as 'techno- panic' is a typical reaction – an intense fear that technologies will impact negatively on society and on youth in particular.[61] Even the Greek philosopher Socrates had concerns about writing upon students, fearing that they would lose the capacity for reason and memory, and since then, there have been techno- panics about the printing press, radio, cinema, magazines, television and, most recently, the internet and, of course, social media. But since its arrival, numerous studies have shown real links between social media usage and poor mental well-being. There is growing evidence that this technology is making some people unhappy – especially those who compare and despair.

The psychologist Leon Festinger described humans as possessing a drive for social comparison in order to develop a sense of self.[62] Virtually everyone engages in social comparison from time to time, but while social comparison may be automatic and unintentional, people vary in the extent to which they engage in this behaviour. Individuals who are excessively socially oriented tend to be insecurely attached and the heaviest users of social media. This is unfortunate because this is the very activity that makes them unhappy. In one study, those who scored the highest in social comparison felt worse about themselves and were more upset when viewing the Facebook page of a friend from the same high school and of the same age and sex.[63] As Gore Vidal quipped, 'Every time a friend succeeds, I die a little.' Envy is a toxic emotion that undermines our happiness.

Whether it's intentional or not, social media encourages people to post their most flattering profiles, experiences and selfies in the expectation that these will garner praise and raise their social standing. But if everyone is posting the best possible version of themselves or highlighting something that others admire, this creates a popularity arms race. Posting only the best moments generates unrealistic representations of people and their lives. If everyone else on social media seems to have a better life, then this would make anyone feel inadequate on at least some dimension – looks, friends, opportunities, jobs, wealth, relationships and so on.

Then there are the more insidious aspects of social media that are – either directly or indirectly – socially aggressive. People behave badly towards others online in ways that they would never dream of doing in person. The impersonality, immediacy and brevity of social media communications makes it too easy to be misinterpreted or to be insensitive to how others will react. Social media polarises arguments into extreme positions, making it difficult to occupy the common ground or find compromise. Then, of course, you could just be ignored – or worse, blocked. Being ignored or excluded on social media may be more upsetting than in real life, because the audience is perceived to be greater – the whole world. Just like the ostracism induced by Cyberball, when we are excluded online, we feel dejected.

The impact of social media on mental health is highly contested, because the negative effects on the whole population may be only minor or negligible overall.[64] However, there has undoubtedly been an exponential rise in the reporting of adolescent mental health problems coinciding with the increase in social media use. This has led to claims, for example by Jonathan Haidt in his book *The Anxious Generation*, that we are in the middle of an epidemic caused by social media rewiring our children's brains.[65] The trouble with this claim is that it is not clear whether the rise is because social media causes mental illness or rather acts like an echo chamber by raising awareness, leading to increased self-diagnosis, reporting, and a corresponding demand for services and treatment.[66] Increased awareness could also bias individuals to interpret any normal variations in mental well-being as being a disorder which then generates self-fulfilling behaviours.[67] In one recent large-scale study,[68] a measure of life satisfaction was applied to over 80,000 UK participants aged ten to eighty years old and was found to be most negatively linked to social media use in the adolescent group of over 17,000 users. Within that group, females showed the strongest negative association with social media use as they entered puberty (eleven to thirteen years of age), whereas the strongest negative relationship in males was several years later (fourteen to fifteen years). Both males and females had a negative peak again at nineteen years of age. Across the entire age range, those who were the most dissatisfied with life were the ones who went on to increase their social media use, thus generating a potential feedback loop to increased unhappiness. This study reveals that individuals who are vulnerable at a time in their life where social status is deemed critically important are most likely to experience the negative impact that social media can generate.

Any activity that corrupts the evolved social dependency and nurturing we require to thrive is a potential risk. Our brains are not matched to this rapidly changing environment that can make us more isolated if we use it unwisely. Most of us will be fine in this brave new world, but as the impact of social media becomes clearer, we must recognise that it represents a real problem for those who are vulnerable. The genie is out of the bottle and so there is no going back, but I expect digital living will eventually come with health warnings and guidelines much as we have with other lifestyle habits that present a risk to well- being.

Technology that encourages us to be more egocentric is a cause for concern. Social media is like fire: it can be used for good, to reach out to others, but it can also destroy if it makes us turn our attention inwards on ourselves. It can become a source of unhappiness when we overvalue the opinions of others and base our sense of worth on our online popularity. Therein lies the real issue of social media. Most of us are concerned about our reputation because we want to be included, valued and not isolated or left alone, which is why social media has become so pervasive in modern life. However, we would be wise to heed the advice of the German philosopher Arthur Schopenhauer, who said, 'Whoever attaches a lot of value to the opinion of others, pays them too much honour.' The problem with that advice is that it fails to acknowledge what a social brain we have evolved and, as we will discover in the next lesson, that social brain is constantly comparing.

Happiness exercises

Invest time in nurturing your relationships. Reach out to someone that you have not spoken to in a long time to rekindle the friendship, or simply drop them a line telling them that you have been thinking about them.

As a parent, encourage healthy social connections between your child and their peers through structured activities such as community events, volunteering, sports and mentorship programmes. It's fine for children to have solitary interests and they should set aside time for scholarly pursuits, but as the saying goes, 'All work and no play' makes for a dull child.

Box-breathe your way out of anxiety. This is a quick remedy for the fight-flight response through controlled breathing. Take note of how quickly you regain control.

Practise a random act of kindness. It doesn't have to be very much. Just a gesture to surprise others into reminding them that we can be kind to each other. Try focusing on an act, as this is one way to amplify the positive experience. Or try recalling when you have been kind in the past to rekindle fond memories.

Take a holiday from social media. Try it for one day and note how this makes you feel. If you must use social media, then set aside and schedule time for it so that it does not encroach upon 'real' time spent with others.

LESSON THREE

Reject Negative Comparisons

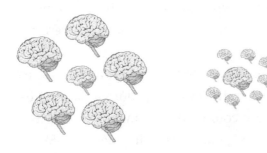

Take a look at the two brains at the centre of each group above and surrounded by the other brains. Does one look larger than the other? If you see the brain on the right as larger than the one on the left, then you are experiencing the Ebbinghaus illusion. In fact, both brains are exactly the same size. Check them with a ruler if you are in doubt. This illusion is created by the neighbouring brains distorting your perception because you automatically calculate a relative comparison and adjust your estimate accordingly. Objects look smaller next to larger objects and larger next to smaller ones.

What do illusions have to do with a book on happiness? Illusions are more than just curiosities of the mind; they remind us that things are not always as they seem. We do not have direct contact with reality. Our reality is something that we assemble because we rarely have access to all of the relevant information and we only process what we can appreciate. It is like the ancient parable of the three blind men and the elephant. Each blind man examines through touch only one small part of the giant beast and so they differ in what they think the creature is. One blind man holding the trunk thinks it's a giant snake, another with the tusk thinks it's a spear, while the one feeling the side thinks it's a wall. We are limited to our own experiences when making judgements, which is why our truths are so subjective. We simply can't see the big picture.

As a state of mind, happiness is entirely subjective and open to interpretation. How we judge our happiness often depends on what we are comparing our mental state with. Am I happier than my neighbour? Am I happier than Elon Musk? This judgement can even depend on which versions of myself I am comparing. Am I happier now compared with when I was a teenager? Am I happier than I was yesterday? It is important to remember that when we are making a judgement, we do so by comparison, and the comparisons we make determine the judgement.

That's not to say that every comparison is a waste of time. There are objective truths in the world that impact on how happy we feel – our status, our salaries, our debts, our grades, our health – but when it comes to evaluating them, we are subjective, especially when it comes to how much they impact on our emotional life. If you ask people what will make them happy, typically wealth, a good job, fame, sex, loving relationships, luxuries and a perfect body come high in the list. These are the things that people want. Some of these satisfy ancient needs for survival. Most are pleasurable, while others establish status. People place a higher priority on some desires than others, but they all suffer from a fundamental flaw: they tend not to make us as happy as we imagine once we have them. This is one of the central claims of the positive psychology movement – namely, that many of the goals we pursue, such as material wealth and fame, do not guarantee sustained happiness.

Can individuals really be so way off in their judgements? Overall, our brains are very efficient and serve us well in interpreting the world to provide information that is valuable to us. However, the human brain has built-in features that can generate distortions that my colleagues and I call 'mindbugs'.[1] These are not necessarily flaws, as they evolved for processing information as efficiently as possible, but they do lead us to make consistent mistakes. The Ebbinghaus brain illusion, where we automatically judge absolute size by making relative comparisons, is one such example of a mindbug. It demonstrates how the brain works by constantly drawing comparisons and reminds us that we exist as a brain in a sea of comparing brains, each operating with a distorted view of reality. If you struggle to adopt another perspective because you are too egocentric, then those comparisons become more distorted. But what if you are wrong about knowing your own mind and the decisions that you believe will make you happy? In this lesson, I want to explore how our judgements of happiness are misconstrued and what we can do about it.

The comparing brain

Every thought, every emotion, every belief and every desire you have plays out in your brain as vast assemblies of nerve cells firing in unison to create the experience of mental life. Every play, every poem, every book, every song, every masterpiece, every brilliant idea or beautifully struck goal conceived by Plato, William Shakespeare, Emily Brontë, Marie Curie, Pelé or any other genius, started out as waves of electrochemical activity cascading across the neural networks that make up the brain.

These nerve cells, the neurons, communicate with each other through nerve impulses or spikes, the language of the brain. What's remarkable is that the basic operation for all neurons is to make comparisons. Our thoughts and actions only transmit when a level of comparison has been achieved. The neuron is effectively a switch that turns on and off depending on whether the other neurons in the network that it is connected to send sufficient signals to activate the switch. When a neuron (let's call it Ronie for short) is at rest, it receives a stream of steady signals from the other neurons it is connected to – a 'Hi Ronie, we're still here, neighbour' kind of message, just to keep in contact. Without these reminders, cells lose their connections and die off. However, when some event – either external or internal – triggers a neural reaction, the neurons connected to each other jump into action. Like dominoes stacked in a row ready to fall, the message cascades as a spreading pattern of activation across the neural networks until it reaches Ronie. However, Ronie won't pass the message on to her connected network until the incoming information reaches a critical threshold, as illustrated below (Fig. 3.1).

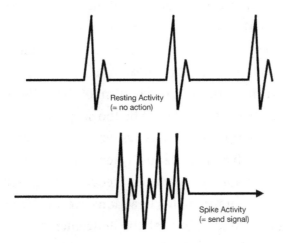

Resting Activity
(= no action)

Spike Activity
(= send signal)

Fig. 3.1: Representation of neuronal activity in a resting stage (top)
and during spike activation (bottom)

At rest, the neuron receives a steady stream of incoming signals until a burst of spike activity reaches a threshold, triggering the cell to send its own signal onto its connected network.

When Ronie does respond, she does so by releasing brain chemicals called *neurotransmitters* that set off the chain reaction in the other neurons she is connected to. In this way, messages traverse the various networks of the brain that control our sensations, perceptions, actions, thoughts and feelings – in other words, all of our mental life.

Once Ronie has sent her signal, she goes back to resting again, waiting for the next big thing to come along. This is the fundamental way our brains work – noticing changes in the world and responding. Compare and contrast – is this incoming signal the same or is it different, and, if so, what is different? It is important to notice a rustle in the bushes or another sudden sound, because it might signal a predator in the undergrowth or an intruder in your house that requires an immediate response. When there are no noticeable changes, situations tend not to be life-threatening.

If comparison is the basic mechanism of the building blocks of the brain, then we should not be too surprised that it operates all the way up the nervous system. Food tastes different depending on what we have just eaten. Pain can be more or less intense depending on what preceded it. From sensations to perceptions, from thoughts to actions, we are drawing constant comparisons to make relative judgements. This is also true of our social status. Our brains are geared to be constantly comparing ourselves with others and, as we learned in the last lesson, our sense of self is established over childhood and is dependent on our relative relationships with others. We want to be included, we want to be liked and we want to have status, and that all depends on how we compare with others. These are the universal motivations that guide our behaviours and choices in life, but the problem is that the comparisons we draw with other people often reach the wrong conclusions. Let's consider why this is the case.

Rules of thumb

Daniel Kahneman and his late colleague psychologist Amos Tversky spent decades demonstrating that the human mind uses shortcuts and rules of thumb when reasoning about the world.[2] These shortcuts, or *heuristics*, reduce the amount of time and effort to make decisions and are generally good estimates of the world. For example, if I ask you to think of a pet, it is likely that you will imagine either a dog or a cat. You're less likely to think of a donkey, a pig or a goat and even less likely to think of a spider or a snake. Many animals can be pets, but the most common pets are cats and dogs. The heuristic operates to choose those members that are most representative of the category of pet animals. Here the representative heuristic works fine. However, it can lead us down the wrong path. For example, try to explain the following scenario:

> A father and his son were involved in a car accident, in which the father was killed and the son was seriously injured. The father was pronounced dead at the scene of the accident and his body was taken to a local morgue. The son was taken by an ambulance to a nearby hospital and was immediately wheeled into an emergency operating theatre. A surgeon was called. Upon arrival and seeing the patient, the attending surgeon exclaimed, 'Oh my God, it's my son!'

If you are like the 40 per cent of people stumped by this scenario, you are probably wondering how the dead father could be about to operate on his son.[3] The obvious explanation is that the surgeon is not the father but the mother. There are female trauma surgeons, but they are not representative of the stereotype when most of us think of surgeons. Here, our rule of thumb fails us.

When we are drawing comparisons to estimate states of mind, we operate with all sorts of heuristics, but these can be faulty and based on incorrect stereotypes. We have all heard that divorce is awful, while having a baby is the most amazing thing that can happen. That may be true for most people, but not for everyone. For some people, divorce is a blessing while having children is not always a great experience, but they are not the majority – or at least that is how it is commonly portrayed. This leads to a general bias to assume that these events are more consistent (divorce is always bad) and more impactful (divorce will leave you bereft) than they really are – a point we address in greater depth in the next lesson, when we consider negative events.

Another mindbug is the availability bias: the tendency to bring to mind for comparison the thoughts that come most easily. When we can visualise or imagine something quickly, this leads us to overestimate the rare and underestimate the common. People fear sharks and aeroplanes, for example, more than they fear bees or cars. The reality is that both bees and cars are far more dangerous than sharks and planes, but because shark attacks and plane crashes are so rare and traumatic, and often make the headlines, they come to mind more easily. Here's another example from Kahneman's *Thinking, Fast and Slow*.[4] What do you think are more common: words that start with the letter K or those that have a K as their third letter? Upon being asked this question, words like 'Kind, Kiss, Kid, Kick' immediately jump to mind, which is why most people think that there are many more words that start with the letter K in the English language than those that have a K as their third letter. In fact, among the most commonly used words, there are approximately twice as many words that have K as a third letter than those that begin with the consonant. But because it is easier to think of words starting with K than those that have it as the third letter, most people overestimate their frequency.

All sorts of biases influence our comparisons, such as the tendency to only notice what we pay attention to (*attentional blindness*), the tendency to seek out and highlight evidence that confirms our beliefs (*confirmation bias*) and the tendency to revise retrospectively our predictions in accordance with the outcomes (*hindsight bias*). As explored in Lesson One, we experience our mental life as a set of constructed narratives, and we like our stories to be coherent and consistent. We change the details to fit with the narrative we wish to create. From the story-telling perspective, we only pay attention to some details while ignoring others, we draw upon expectations and we make predictions about what we think will happen based on previous experience, but those experiences are distorted and misremembered. Even some of the most memorable and impactful life events, such as winning an Olympic medal, are distorted by mindbugs and heuristics.

Adulation of the audience

Imagine your pride, standing on the podium and watching as your country's flag is raised to the roar of the Olympic crowd. All those years of practice, pain and dedication are finally paying off as your success is recognised at the greatest sporting event in the world. However, it is not always a happy time for all the medalists. In an influential study of the medalists in the 1992 Barcelona Olympics, researchers noted that the silver medalists were particularly unhappy with their success.[5] When they reviewed the video footage of the points in the contest when 1) they discover their medal placing and 2) the actual award ceremony, it was noted on both occasions that the happiest athletes were the gold-medal winners and the bronze-medal winners, with second-placed athletes the least happy, as indicated by their smiling and body language. This was especially true if the bronze finalists did not have medal expectations, compared with silver medalists with gold-medal dreams. Like a real version of the Ebbinghaus illusion, silver medalists were comparing themselves with the gold medalists, who had greater success, in a 'what could have been' moment, rather than comparing themselves with the bronze medalists. In contrast, the bronze medalists who did not expect to be standing on the podium were comparing their success with that of all the other competitors who didn't even get a medal.

The Olympic medal placings should provide an objective measure of performance, and yet there is still subjective variation in our responses. Now imagine how much more problematic it will be if you compete on measures that are much harder to define, such as success in life or relationships. Unlike the metrics of Olympic performance such as speed, seconds, pounds or distances, measuring success in life is much more subjective.

When we reflect on our failures and successes, who are we comparing ourselves with? On every imaginable dimension of success, there are individuals who seem to be doing better than us. We tend to draw our comparisons with those who are most like us, but even then, we pick and choose our comparisons. Do you compare your relationship success with your best friend but then your professional success to your work manager? We rarely have full insight to other people's lives and make assumptions. The problem is that if you pick and choose different individuals to compare yourself with, then you will ultimately find that there is always someone who is doing better. And even those you regard as objectively successful can always imagine another more successful person with whom to compare themselves. This is the problem with an overly egocentric perspective. As you are the centre of attention, you compare yourself with others rather than seeing the relative comparisons that exist between others. I will feel inadequate if I compare myself with individual top academics, athletes, businesspeople, actors, celebrities or anyone else who features prominently in culture or comes to mind easily. What I will fail to appreciate is that everyone in these categories will also feel inadequate, depending on the comparisons they draw. Then, of course, there are all the problems that successful people experience that we are not aware of. Nobody's life is perfect. All we see when we make the comparisons is someone who has achieved more than we have on some dimension of achievement, ability, looks, popularity and so on.

This is not to say we should avoid comparison altogether. Competition can be good in propelling us to reach our potential. In one of the earliest social psychology experiments, published in 1898, Norman Triplett, an early cycling enthusiast, noted that a rider's track times were faster when they competed against others rather than racing against the clock.[6] To test this effect of competition in an experiment, Triplett had children compete on an apparatus where they have to reel in rods to catch as many fish as possible in a game he devised to measure performance. Compared with when they were playing the game alone, children were faster when there was another child present. This phenomenon is called *social facilitation* and is not limited to humans but can be found throughout the animal kingdom. Animals run faster, eat more quicky and generally up their game when there are others around.

Social facilitation enhances performance by providing a tangible opponent who represents a goal to aim for and beat, but it turns out that even the presence of an audience will raise our game. If we can adopt the allocentric perspective, then we can benefit from the team effort. We may take less personal credit for successes, but this is then offset by the advantages of not being solely responsible for any failings. The dynamics of solo versus group performance are complicated, as any good coach will know.

For social facilitation to work, however, you need to feel competent and confident, because an audience can impair performance in a phenomenon known as *choking*.[7] This happens when our nerves get the better of us and, in these situations, performance anxiety is counterproductive. This is our fight-flight response overacting again. When it comes to the penalty shoot-out in the World Cup finals, it is not necessarily the most skilled striker who is the one who should be taking the shot, but, rather, the one who will not crack under the pressure.

Despite our problematic comparisons with famous and successful people, normally we tend to view our own personal attributes in a more positive light when comparing with others. In other words, we tend to think we are better than others, but not necessarily better *off* than others. Again, this is the egocentric child within us. In Lesson One we noted that preschoolers are prone to exaggerate their attributes because they lack the experience and mental machinery to draw more accurate comparisons. As adults, we may be more modest, but most of us still have an over-inflated sense of importance. Most of us think we possess above-average intelligence, humour, good looks, trustworthiness and morality. These are just some of the positive illusions that many of us carry around in our heads and that keep us happy.[8] Statistically, of course, it is *impossible* for everyone to be above average.

To make matters worse, we regard others as more biased in their opinions, whereas we consider ourselves to be more objective. 'You might *think* you are above average, but I *know* I am!' In this way we defend our vulnerable egos. But one area where we constantly underestimate ourselves is the extent to which we consider how fortunate we are. The reason that many feel hard done by is that we believe we possess above-average abilities that are not appreciated or recognised by others. In a 2022 survey of 2,000 US workers, 63 per cent felt unappreciated and around the same proportion (59 per cent) said they had never had an appreciative boss.[9] This is the egocentric self at play again. We rarely take an objective view to consider our fortune against those who are less fortunate. Rather, we have the tendency to underplay or resent the success of others, which can lead to jealousy and envy, the common bedfellows of an overly active ego.

Because I'm worth it

Wealth is one area where jealousy and envy rear their ugly heads. For my students and, I suspect, much of the population, money is an important goal, but surprisingly it's not the actual amount you get but, rather, the relative amount that determines whether you are happy. In 1995, 257 Harvard faculty staff and students were asked to choose between two hypothetical salary scenarios.[10] Would they prefer Job A, where they earn $50K while their colleagues earn $25K, or Job B, where they earn $100K and their colleagues earn $250K? Over half of the respondents (56 per cent) said they would prefer Job A, even though they would be earning half of what they would be earning in Job B. Although far from an overwhelming majority, it is still surprising that just over half of us would forego absolute value in favour of relative position. The same is true for housing. People would prefer to have a smaller house so long as it was the largest on the street.

In his book of the same name, Robert Frank calls this bias for relative position 'choosing the right pond' because we think it is better to be a big frog in a small pond than a small frog in a big pond.[11] The problem with this strategy is how do you estimate the size of the pond? We are notoriously bad at accurately estimating how we compare with others. Most people believe that they are not being valued enough. A survey of over 71,000 employees in a large software company found that two thirds (64 per cent) thought that they were being underpaid even though they were earning the market rate for their job.[12] Of those who were being paid a salary higher than the average market rate, only one fifth (21 per cent) recognised that they were on a good salary. These discrepancies led to a second problem: those who believed that they were underpaid were not happy in their employment and more likely to seek another job. What is interesting is that much of this resentment can be removed if the actual pay that everyone receives is made public. This indicates that what we *imagine* plays a greater role in our disaffection than the *reality*, because we are so way off in our assumptions about what everyone else is being paid.

Reject Negative Comparisons

If our comparisons are the basis of our happiness, it would be fair to assume that our circumstances will play a role in our perception. This leads to the prediction that we will be happier if there is less obvious discrepancy between the 'haves' and the 'have-nots'. It is well established that unemployment is associated with poor mental well-being, but it depends on whether you are living in an area of high unemployment. If you look at levels of well-being and economic status across England organised by postcode, those who are most unhappy are the unemployed who live in areas of high employment.[13] If everyone around you is doing well, that makes you feel inadequate. However, if you are unemployed and you live in an area where unemployment is the norm, then you will have higher mental well-being because everyone is in the same situation, so there is no need to feel comparatively worse off. What's surprising, however, is that you also tend to feel better than those who are employed and living in an area of high unemployment. Why might that be? Counterintuitively, having a job when everyone around you is unemployed doesn't make you feel better. We may be egocentric, but we still want to be accepted even when we are comparatively better off. Who you compare yourself with also explains why unemployed people report a substantial increase in happiness when they reach retirement age, even though their objective level of standard-of-living has not changed.[14] The reason for this is that not working is no longer a violation of the social norm of employment, and so contentment increases because most people of your age are now in the same boat.

Party animals

Who goes to more parties – you or other people? If you are like most normal people, you will answer that you don't go to as many parties as other people. This is another blind spot in our self-conception of how we compare with others, in the extent to which we live enriched social lives. Most of us feel comparatively lonely, which, as we have seen, is a potentially unhealthy social situation. In 2022, only 20 per cent, or one in five, said they never feel lonely, according to the UK Office for National Statistics.[15] While actual social isolation does indeed predict vulnerability to illness, it is important to recognise that this is also true of *perceived* loneliness. You can be a popular person with a wide social network but still feel lonely, which has negative consequences for your mental and physical health. But estimates of our own loneliness are distorted because of the unrealistic comparisons we draw with others. In one study, people were asked the party question alongside related additional questions about going out to dinner, having friends, wider social networks and frequent interactions with family.[16] On average, people believed that they went to fewer parties, had fewer friends, smaller social networks and went out to dine less than other people.

Again, like our inaccurate estimates of being above average intelligence, equally, not everyone can be below the average when it comes to sociability. Why this distortion? The reason is that when asked to make a comparison on a vague notion, people think of the most available concept of what a social person is. It's the shark problem again. They imagine a party animal, maybe a celebrity socialite who actively and willingly tells us how big their social circles are. By that comparison, most of us are going to look relatively unsociable. This creates an 'anchoring' problem because we make the wrong comparison, tying our estimate to the first unrealistic model that comes to mind.

Anchoring is a well-known mindbug in human reasoning that arises from comparisons. When people try to make estimates or predictions, they begin with some initial value or starting point and then adjust from there. For example, if you ask individuals to perform mental multiplication rapidly without a calculator, then the starting numbers will influence their estimate. If you start with the equation 8 x 7 x 6 x 5 x 4 x 3 x 2 x 1 = ?, the mean value people estimate for the product is 2,250; whereas others presented with the same problem in reverse – 1 x 2 x 3 x 4 x 5 x 6 x 7 x 8 = ? – think that the answer is only 512. Of course, they are the same equation and in fact both answers are way off – the correct answer is actually a much higher figure of 40,320. The reason for the difference is that, in the first instance, the initial value anchors the estimate to 8 x 7 – larger numbers that lead to a greater prediction compared with the second instance, starting with 1 x 2.

Anchoring is the reason that most people choose the mid-range price of wine at a restaurant. The wine that people end up choosing depends on what is the most expensive one on the list. And when we look to make a purchase, we are most likely to choose an item that has been marked down from a much greater recommended retail price (RRP) because it represents a better bargain, even though this reduction is a simple anchoring ploy. For example, the RRP is only a suggested price and so when the retailer displays a price that is below the RRP, the customer assumes it is a bargain. If on the other hand, transactions typically involve haggling such as buying a new car, then retailers will display prices above the RRP so that when the price is negotiated downwards, the customer believes they have successfully achieved a bargain. Again, the take-home point is that our interpretations based on comparison are fraught with subjective biases and this has major implications for how we estimate our happiness.

If anchoring is clouding our comparisons when it comes to judging our social lives, which in turn makes us underestimate our activities, then we should be able to shift the rating by changing the anchor. To test this, in a second follow-up study to the party survey, participants were asked to compare themselves with those who lead particularly vibrant social lives, while others were asked to compare themselves with those who lead particularly poor social lives. Under these two different conditions, those who were asked to imagine the party animal first gave the same inadequate underestimates as previously found in the first study. However, those who were asked the same question but compared themselves with those who were lonely showed a reduction in the bias to assume that they led a socially impoverished life. Together, these two findings show that, left to our own devices, we compare upwards like the silver medalists. We naturally think of those we imagine doing so much better than ourselves, which makes us feel inadequate. However, when we are made to become more allocentric or at least aware of those below our social standing, we can become more realistic if we broaden our perspective to consider those who are less fortunate. We can be more like the bronze medalists, content to be on the podium of life.

We can now use our understanding of the comparison and anchoring mindbugs to generate a happiness hack that will be familiar to most of us. Gratitude is when we notice and appreciate the positive things in the world. We can be grateful for others who have helped us, for the everyday pleasures in life or simply for being alive. The Roman philosopher Cicero called gratitude 'not only the greatest of virtues, but also the parent of the others'. This is because gratitude promotes happiness by focusing on the positive rather than negative things in our lives. We can be grateful for colleagues, partners and significant others in our lives. When we are grateful for others, it strengthens our social bonds and also reminds us of our achievement and self-worth because we are made to recognize appropriate social comparisons. In turn, this gratitude encourages us to help and support others. Also, we cannot be jealous or envious when we are grateful, and so our social comparisons are more positive. When we think about being grateful, we are forced to acknowledge what we are lucky to have, and this should trigger comparisons with those who do not have. This draws us to make a downward comparison, making us realise how fortunate we are and focus less on what we feel we are lacking. Finally, being grateful reminds us to count our blessings, which helps combat 'adaptation', another mindbug that we'll address next.

Adaptation

If our friendly neuron, Ronie, and her gang receive consistent repeated signals, they eventually get used to it. This is called *adaptation*. There are a number of reasons for adaptation. First, it is metabolically costly to keep responding to a repeated signal, as each nerve impulse requires energy. As we noted earlier, the brain is metabolically hungry. It may be only 2 per cent of the total body weight but it requires 20 per cent of the total energy we consume each day. Second, unchanging signals are not informative, as it is business as usual. Finally, to detect a new signal, you need to reset back to the resting level so that you can register any changes.

Perception provides clear examples of adaptation. If you are outside on a bright summer's day and then enter a darkened room, at first you can't see anything clearly. This is because in the bright light outside, the receptors in your eyes adjust to the levels of light, so when you enter the darkened room, you have to now adapt to lower light levels before you can begin to see what's inside. If you go outside again, then you are blinded by the brightness because you adapted to the dark room. What is true of the receptors in your eyes is also true of neurons that code for all experiences. We adapt to everything, whether it is listening to the same music track, hearing the same story or eating the same food, day after day. Our brains rapidly learn to get used to things.

The problem is that we rarely consider how much adaptation will flatten our future happiness. When you are hungry and crave calories, you might decide to buy the extra-large tub of rocky-road ice cream. You salivate and imagine how delicious it will be. You think you will enjoy that tub of ice cream until it is finished, but after a few mouthfuls you become satiated and start to get sick of it. All experiences are subject to adaptation because the brain registers changes in experiences rather than steady states. Imagine what your world would be like if you never got used to new experiences. Your brain would be overwhelmed very quickly as your mind filled up with the cacophony of information.

Take a moment to be mindful of your current range of experiences. Begin by noticing the pressure of the ground on the soles of your feet, or the hardness of the seat against your backside. Can you feel the clothing against your body? What about the pressure of your tongue inside your mouth? Can you now hear all the external noises? What can you smell?

When you become aware of the all the potential sensory experiences that you don't normally notice, it becomes clear that there is a lot that you are getting used to. And that's just the sensory messages coming into your brain. Imagine how full your mind would become if you had to add all the thoughts for the day, things to be done and other mental messages that need some attention. Clearly, you don't want to pay attention to everything at once as you would become overwhelmed very quickly and incapable of doing anything. We normally cope with such potential overload of sensory and mental information by processes of adaptation and attention, but it's what you choose to pay attention to that determines your happiness.

If you want to get the maximum happiness from an event or experience, amplify the positive by focusing your attention. Savouring is a positive psychology technique to get the maximum enjoyment out of pleasurable experiences. We are often in such a hurry that we fail to notice and benefit from the familiar pleasures that our brains have adapted to. Food provides a good example. To reinstate the pleasure of eating, take extra time to really savour the experience by focusing your attention on the minute details such as taste and texture. Make it last as long as possible. Slow down and chew every mouthful.

But with our brain constantly comparing and adapting, we struggle to achieve sustained happiness and soon get used to any emotional benefit we get. This leads to a relentless pursuit known as the *hedonic treadmill*.[17] Hedonic because we are seeking happiness, and a treadmill because no matter how much we pursue it, we never really get there.

Some good news is that the hedonic treadmill works both ways. In a classic study[18] led by psychologist Philip Brickman, who first coined the term, researchers looked at the happiness of lottery winners and paralysed accident victims, and concluded that these life-changing events had comparatively little impact on the long-term happiness of the individuals involved because of adaptation. This is a shock to most of us who play the lottery and dread paralysis. It turns out that Brickman probably underestimated the impact of winning the lottery (it does tend to make you happier, especially if you could really do with the money) but he was right that such life-changing events play less of a role in our long-term happiness than we predict.[19] The negative impact of permanent paralysis is also less than we imagine. For example, a survey of 231 patients with spinal cord injuries found that most report themselves to be happy for most of the time, with only 10 per cent responding that they were infrequently happy or not at all.[20] Patients with chronic disabilities report that their quality of life is significantly better than the public estimates that it would be.[21] Why is this?

Predicting what will make us happy

In his bestseller *Stumbling on Happiness*,[22] my colleague social psychologist Dan Gilbert makes the point that while we are generally good at knowing what will make us happy (good food, job, partner) compared with what will make us unhappy (hunger, lousy job, separation), we fail miserably in predicting how much happiness or unhappiness these events will generate and how long these feelings will last. He calls this *affective forecasting* – predicting how we will feel in the future.[23] For any positive or negative situation or life event, you can ask people to predict how much impact these will have and for how long. If you go out and find people who have undergone these life-changing events, you can ask how much impact these events have had and measure how long the impact has lasted. Irrespective of the situation or event, if you compare the prediction with the actual experience, you typically get a mismatch between prediction and outcome. People overestimate the impact of an event and how long it will last – especially when the event is negative, which we will describe in greater depth in the next lesson.

In one study, two weeks before sitting an exam, students were asked, 'Suppose you get a grade that is lower than you expect. During the week after you find out your grade, in general, how happy will you feel?'[24] Students then rated how happy they would feel if they received the grade they expected, and if they instead received a higher grade than they expected. The pattern generally showed that students predicted that they would be happy with a mark that matched or exceeded their expectations, but unhappy with a grade below what they had predicted. After the exam and the marks were given out, the researchers found that after receiving their mark, all students reached the same levels of happiness, irrespective of whether the mark matched their expectations.

Maybe students haven't experienced enough failure to make accurate predictions about the anticipated impact of setbacks. If so, then you might think that repeatedly failing exams should make you better prepared for how you will feel. For example, fewer than half of drivers pass their test on their first attempt. A driving test should provide you with enough experience to accurately predict how you will react if you fail or pass the test on the next attempt. In a study of bad drivers who repeatedly failed their driving tests, it was found that there was no change in their predictions about how they would feel between attempts.[25] Test failers overestimated how long they would feel disappointed but this expectation did not change with repeated failures. The pattern was exactly the same for the drivers who failed one test compared with the really bad drivers who failed the test more than four times. We do not readily learn from experience when it comes to our emotions.

Fear of failure is one of the most pressing problems in today's education system. I see this all the time with my university students who are so anxious about failing that they worry themselves sick. However much I can tell them that whatever the outcome, it will not be as bad as they imagine in the long term, it makes little impact on their anxiety. What's more worrying is that it is no longer simply a fear of failing but, increasingly, the desire to seek top marks because they regard anything below the class average as substandard.

Failure is underestimated as an important learning experience. It not only teaches humility, but tells us something about our resolve – our willingness to not give up. To demonstrate this in class, I have an exercise for my students. I ask them, Who wants to be an entrepreneur? Typically, a large proportion of hands rise, as many at this age seek to be independently wealthy. I then explain that most businesses require venture capital (VC) investment and that often requires pitching your start-up proposal to investors. I then present the students with the following question: 'If you are an investor and two individuals pitch business plans that are equally attractive, which would you choose? The successful entrepreneur who has never failed or the one who has failed repeatedly?' Most assume that the successful entrepreneur will be preferred because they have a track record of starting a successful company, until the students learn that almost all businesses are doomed to failure within the first couple of years. As an investor, you want to back the entrepreneur who has the grit and experience to overcome the likely challenges they will face. If you are lucky enough to have a successful start-up, then you remain untested. However, if you are someone who can get over the failure, dust yourself off and try again, then that demonstrates the necessary resilience to overcome whatever curveballs life will inevitably throw at you. Maybe this experience explains why entrepreneurs coming off an initial VC-backed failure often see their careers accelerate in their follow-on jobs.[26]

There are positive lessons to be learned from failure. Try the following exercise. Write down something that you have failed at in your life. It could be an exam. It could be business. It could be a relationship. We have all failed at something at some time in our lives. Describing a time when you failed is a common interview question because it reveals important insights about a candidate's humility, resilience and ability to learn. Next, write down something good that came out of that failure. Something that probably would not have happened if you had not failed. You should be able to find other opportunities that arose only because of your setback. Maybe you took a different career path or found your current partner. This exercise teaches us that we can overcome adversity and all things come to pass with time. It also gives us a long-term perspective that is often lacking at the time we think that our world is falling apart.

Focalism

Why do we fail to accurately predict the future? Adaptation is one major mindbug, but there is another that is less obvious. In fact, we often don't spot it. Let me demonstrate with a bit of mind control (Fig. 3.2). Freely pick one of the cards opposite – though whether you believe it or not, I am going to influence your decision before you have made your choice. Which one are you going to choose? Take a moment, but once you have decided on a card, focus on that card and remember it before reading on.

Fig. 3.2: Pick a card, any card.

Although you think you chose your card freely, I did, in fact, control your decision, and I am going to remove the card you picked. If you look below (Fig. 3.3), you will see that the card you chose has been removed.

Figure 3.3: The card you chose has magically been removed.
Read on to discover how.

Am I a mind-reader, or a Svengali who can control your thought processes? If only. After a moment's consideration – or you might simply check back – you will realise that not only has your card been removed but so have all of the other original cards!

It is remarkable how many people are fooled by this simple trick. Magic relies on psychology and an understanding of the

97

limits of our attentional systems. When we focus our attention, we do so to the exclusion of noticing other things. Both magicians and pickpockets deliberately manipulate us to focus our attention in one direction while they surreptitiously hide a rabbit or steal our possessions. Misdirection reveals the limits of our attention, but even without deliberate manipulation, we are simply not equipped to pay attention to everything going on. This leads to *focalism*, the tendency to notice only what we are paying attention to.

Focalism is a contributing factor in affective forecasting. When we predict how an event will impact on our future self, we narrow our focus on that event alone in isolation and do not consider all the other things that might change in the future that will have mitigating effects.[27] We might imagine that paralysis will be terrible because we concentrate on everything that an able-bodied person will lose and find it difficult to imagine what could possibly make up for that loss.[28] Focalism also blinds us to the unforeseen consequences that arise as a result of a major life event. Think about winning the lottery again. Yes, this win would remove many of your financial concerns, but suddenly coming into a large sum of money can also have negative effects.[29] It could, for example, change your behaviour by increasing unhealthy habits such as smoking and alcohol consumption. Infamously, the nineteen-year-old UK lottery winner Michael Carroll blew his £9.7 million fortune on drink, drugs and brothels, which left him divorced and penniless. (His wife remarried him once his fortune had disappeared.) Winning the lottery can also change those around you. In a study of Dutch lottery winners who won a new car, their neighbours were much more likely to buy a new car, in a keeping-up-with-the-Joneses effect.[30] Hardly a recipe for harmony if you are competing against your neighbour for status. In 1988, William Post won $16.2 million in the Pennsylvania Lottery. Shortly afterwards, his brother tried to hire a hitman to kill him in an attempt to inherit the money. The hit never happened but Post died eighteen years later, penniless, $1 million in debt and living off food stamps. His is not the only story of misfortune that comes from winning a fortune.[31]

By focusing on just one aspect of our lives, we are failing to consider all the other things that contribute to happiness. For example, if you ask students two questions, 'How happy are you with your life in general?' followed by 'How many dates did you have last month?', there is absolutely no relationship between the answers.[32] However, if you reverse the order of the questions and start with the dating question, this produces a strong relationship. Those with more dates rate themselves as happier with their lives compared with those who went on fewer dates. By focusing (and anchoring) the respondent to a measure of popularity, you are influencing their subsequent evaluation of well-being. The same effect can be found when attention is first called to a respondent's marriage or their health. The reason happiness levels change is that people do not know how happy they are in general and so they become susceptible to the focusing of attention on different aspects of their life. When people consider the impact of any single factor on their happiness, they are prone to exaggerate its importance.

The chase

Sometimes we are so focused on the pursuit of happiness that we fail to appreciate that it is the pursuit and the anticipation which is really motivating us. For many, anticipating that reward is where the pleasure is most intense, especially if you have to wait for it. This is supported by classic learning theory that demonstrates that intermittent rewards produce stronger learning because of the infrequent and unpredictable nature of the reinforcement.[33] If we always immediately got what we wanted, we would adapt very quickly and our motivation would be lost. The power of anticipation in reward is supported by a neurotransmitter, *dopamine*, that has entered popular culture as a so-called pleasure chemical.

Dopamine is active in the brain's reward centres that generate pleasure, but contrary to popular belief, it is not the basis for happiness. People talk about getting a 'dopamine hit' from various activities such as shopping or receiving praise from online social media validation as if it were a psychoactive drug like heroin or cocaine, but that is not how dopamine works. This myth can be traced back to early animal studies in the 1950s that found that rats would repeatedly press a lever to deliver electrical stimulation to the reward centres of the brain.[34] This became so addictive that they would press the lever up to 2,000 times per hour. The lever-pressing activated the brain centres where dopamine operates, implicating the neurotransmitter as the basis for *hedonia* because animals would forego basic drives such as food in order to self-stimulate.[35] Also, humans with profound depression who experienced little joy in life had lower levels of dopamine,[36] which is how the neurotransmitter earned the reputation for being the happiness or pleasure chemical.[37] However, the problem with this idea is that subsequent studies have shown that knocking out the release of dopamine in genetically modified mice does not change the pleasure or preferences that animals experience.[38] If you remove dopamine-producing cells, mice still get pleasure from food; they simply won't go and get it. Human studies have been even more controversial than the rodent studies. In one unethical study to 'cure' psychiatric patients of homosexual tendencies, an electrode implanted deep in the brain to the same dopaminergic reward centres produced increased lever-pressing but, rather than delivering pleasure, it was more likely it generated simply an urge to press the lever.[39]

Dopamine is more to do with the pursuit than the pleasure itself. If something you do is enjoyable, then it becomes associated with a release of dopamine, which reminds the brain that this delivers a pleasurable experience. The consequence is that you're more likely to repeat that behaviour again. This distinction has been addressed by neuropsychologist Vaughan Bell,[40] who describes the neurotransmitter like a 'could have been' commentator pointing out the successes, but also the near misses. This explains why dopamine is equally active in gamblers when they lose money as when they win.[41] So, it can't really be a pleasure chemical unless you like losing. In many ways, dopamine has less to do with pleasure or happiness and more to do with wanting.

Wanting is a powerful drive. When asked if they would prefer $10 now or $30 in three months' time, most people opt for the immediate reward. This is called *delayed discounting*. Given the choice, most of us would prefer a reward sooner rather than later, and the longer the delay, the less we want the future reward.[42] The next time you feel that you must have something because you think that it will make you happy, ask yourself this question: 'Do I really need this now or can it wait?' Try introducing a decision delay to determine whether your desire fades away with time. You could set yourself a timer of thirty minutes on your phone before making a decision or you could imagine a future self: ask yourself how much you'd like something now, and then imagine how much you will like it in three months' time. Both methods introduce a real or imagined time-out to reflect.

We often want things because we believe that we will like what we get, and this will make us happier. However, psychologists Dan Gilbert and his collaborator Timothy Wilson have identified that there is often a mismatch between what we want and what we like.[43] For example, we may want a holiday and find that it doesn't turn out to be as much fun as we had anticipated. Of course, there are times when the holiday exceeds our expectations, but Gilbert and Wilson argue that we are often incorrect at predicting what will make us happy in a phenomenon they call *miswanting.*

Miswanting is another example of the failure of affective forecasting. Sometimes we simply incorrectly want something that will not make us happy. Probably, the most unexpected example of miswanting is choice. We assume – often wrongly – that we would always prefer more choices because we would like to have more control over our lives. Too many choices, however, can be counterproductive and stressful. Shoppers confronted with the choice of thirty different varieties of jam or gourmet chocolates are more likely to walk away without buying any, compared with when they are presented with only half a dozen choices. If employees are given a free trip to Paris, they are happy. If you give them a free trip to Hawaii, they are happy. But if you offer them the choice between the two destinations, they are less happy, no matter what they choose. Why might choice be so disruptive?

The reason is that choice forces us to make comparisons and acknowledge relative disadvantages. People who choose Paris complain that it doesn't have the ocean and those who choose Hawaii regret that it doesn't have the museums. Psychologist Barry Schwartz calls this the 'tyranny of choice' because rather than providing freedom, it actually constrains our decision-making.[44] He argues that greater choice increases unhappiness because we fret that we are going to make the wrong decision and so we get stressed about trying to process all the comparisons in an effort to get it right. This both increases our fear of making the wrong choice and raises expectations that we should be able to get the best choice. Having made the choice, we then start to regret, wondering whether it was the right one.

According to Schwartz, excessive choice is one of the reasons that there are increasing levels of unhappiness reported in the affluent West. To test this counterintuitive claim, Schwartz and his colleagues administered a self-report survey[45] that asked a series of statements to select that were related to decision behaviour, such as 'I often find it difficult to shop for a gift for a friend' or 'No matter how satisfied I am with my job, it's only right for me to be on the lookout for better opportunities.' Individuals were asked to rate these statements about themselves on a scale of 1 to 7 (from 'completely disagree' to 'completely agree'). The researchers then divided the group into those who they described as 'maximisers', who had the highest ratings for making comparisons, to the lowest scorers, called 'satisficers', who stopped comparing as soon as they had found an item that satisfied their requirements.

Maximisers expended considerable effort and energy to make the right choice – reading labels, comparing prices etc. – whereas satisficers were much quicker to make a decision. When it came to being happy with their choice, maximisers were more likely to express regrets and be unhappy with a purchase, with increased brooding and rumination. Maximisers tend to be people who are more prone to regret; they are less satisfied with life, less optimistic and more depressed than satisficers. The reason for this, as we will discover in the next lesson, is that regret weighs more heavily in our minds than satisfaction.

If you find choice overwhelming, then probably the best way to curtail the negative maximiser mindset is to limit the opportunity for choice in the first place. Identify your core requirements and set out to make a limited maximum number of comparisons. For example, only compare five items and rank them in order of worst to best. Once you have done this, stop searching and settle on your final choice. If you should later start to have regrets, make the comparison between your final choice and the worst one on the list rather than with the second best. That way the benefits will be more obvious.

Armed with our comparing brain, we are constantly seeking positive goals and futures to improve our relative position. What we want, what we pursue, the control we seek and the choices we make are all geared towards greater happiness, but each of these can be undermined by different types of mind-bugs. Probably the biggest mindbug of all is our bias towards negativity: the subject of the next lesson.

Happiness exercises

Write down three things in your life that you are grateful for. When we think about gratitude, we are forced to recognise that not everyone is so fortunate, and this encourages us to make downward comparisons instead of the upward comparisons that bring us so much unhappiness.

Practise savouring to combat adaptation. Take your time and focus on the pleasure that an activity provides. If you're eating a meal, slowly enjoy the flavours and textures. Focus your attention on the sensory aspects of pleasure, in whatever ways you may achieve it.

Acknowledge the times when you have failed in life. But recognise how you have overcome setbacks and include some of the unforeseen positive things that may have arisen from these failures. Write down three things that you have failed at but then the unexpected gains from these setbacks – for example, new job opportunities, new relationships or other positive outcomes.

Remember that wanting is not the same as liking. Try to recognise when you feel impulsive. Take time out before making a major decision such as an expensive purchase, or try to imagine how you will feel about your choice later in time. Give some consideration to the situation so that you feel more comfortable with your decision. If it is the wrong decision, then at least you cannot be accused of being too impulsive.

LESSON FOUR

Become More Optimistic

People are unrealistic about the future. A poll by YouGov in 2016 revealed that 65–70 per cent of US and UK respondents thought that, all things considered, the world was getting worse, with only 4–6 per cent thinking it was getting better.[1] However, the opposite is true. On just about every measure of human well-being, data proves that things are much better now than they were in the past. Personal wealth, standards of living and life expectancy have all improved over recent history, and there is less violence against individuals and fewer wars.[2]

Although there is widespread pessimism about the world, most of us are more optimistic when it comes to our own personal futures. In a 2005 study,[3] participants were instructed: 'Please imagine a ladder with steps numbered from zero at the bottom to ten at the top. The top of the ladder represents the best possible life for you, and the bottom of the ladder represents the worst. On which step do you think you will stand about five years from now?' When this future-oriented question was administered to over 150,000 representative citizens from 142 countries, the most common response was a seven on the ladder and the average for the entire world sample was 6.7, with only one country, Zimbabwe, scoring below the mid-point range of five. Clearly people across the world tend to be universally optimistic when it comes to predicting their own futures five years down the road.

Personal optimism is the norm when it comes to imagining our distant futures, but as the neuroscientist Tali Sharot has argued, in some areas of our lives we can be overly optimistic.[4] For example, consider marriage and the expectation to 'live happily ever after'. Even though the statistics clearly show that currently around 40–50 per cent of UK and US marriages will end in divorce, couples do not think that applies to them. And that includes newly married divorce lawyers, who should know better![5] Oscar Wilde once quipped, 'Marriage is the triumph of imagination over intelligence. Second marriage is the triumph of hope over experience.' This optimism bias also explains why we tend to ignore health-risk warnings, underestimate the costs and time to complete projects and think that we are unlikely to be burgled or involved in a car accident. For most people, such future events seem distant and unlikely.

It's not too surprising that people expect a better future for themselves. Indeed, we need to imagine better futures. Otherwise, we would not be motivated by the prospect of becoming happier. We would not marry if we believed that we would get divorced. We would not apply for a job or for a promotion if we didn't think we could get it. But how can we simultaneously hold two seemingly contradictory beliefs, that the future of the world is negative (as noted at the start of this lesson) but we think the future for ourselves is positive? And if we are generally optimistic about our own long-term future, then why are happiness levels on the decline from year to year? How can you be generally optimistic about your future but unhappy about your current situation at the same time?

The answer is that we can be both optimistic and pessimistic, depending on what time frame we are considering. In fact, as we shall see, optimism and pessimism may actually be two separate components of personality. Also, we vary on a sliding scale on both dimensions, which is why you shouldn't label someone simply as either an optimist or a pessimist. People are more complex and nuanced than that. We can imagine that things will get better in some aspects of our lives, but not necessarily others, and so we can still consider ourselves unhappy overall, especially if we make the unrealistic comparisons we addressed in the last lesson.

In this lesson, we consider how to be happier by becoming more optimistic about the world, ourselves and others, because there are tangible benefits to doing so. Not only are optimists happier, but they are healthier, better liked and live longer. Multiple studies that have looked for individual differences on numerous dimensions to predict health outcomes find that time and time again, optimism comes out as the consistent beneficial factor.[6] How can positive minds produce healthier bodies? Let's investigate some of the mechanisms that may be at play here.

Optimism is about anticipating brighter futures. To do that we need to understand what gets in the way of our ability to think more positively in the present and how to change our outlook. It may be challenging to always look on the bright side of life when we view the world so negatively, but the good news from the Science of Happiness is that it is possible to change. To do so, we must recognise what sort of information we attend to when thinking about the world, ourselves and others, and the way that we are biased to process it. Once we understand our biases, we can learn and practise techniques to imagine better futures and to view our current situations more positively. If you're feeling stuck in your pessimistic perception of the world, you can learn to become more optimistic.

Bad is stronger than good

The first challenge to becoming more optimistic is to understand the nature of information and the way we process it. Many animals, including humans, have evolved a propensity to pay special attention and overreact to negative signals in the environment.[7] This includes information from the past, present and future.

In the present, we are faster to respond to negative sounds, words, voices and faces. Take a look at the faces below (Fig. 4.1) and see if you can spot the odd one out.

Fig. 4.1: Spot the odd one out. (Adapted from Fox et al., 2000)

There are in fact two odd faces here. If we are presented with a sea of faces, then we are generally quicker to spot an angry face than a happy face in the crowd.[8] The same is true of voices. When we are yelled at, our brains respond much faster, with more intensity, than when we hear happy or neutral voices.[9] This priority operates from an early age. Infants react more strongly to angry voices than positive voices, especially from parents.[10] Negative signals are more effective in stopping us in our tracks, which is useful in avoiding danger. They trigger the freeze component that usually kicks in before the flight-or-fight response. There is no equivalent positive signal that can operate so strongly.

Hyper-awareness of negative signals is essential for young infants, who have much to discover about the world. When young children find themselves in an unfamiliar situation or encounter something new, they will look towards others to determine how they should respond, and the messages that are most easily understood are negative.[11] For example, when presented with a toy they have never seen before, one-year-olds take their lead from their mother, looking to her for reassurance. If mum looks at it with an expression of disgust and talks about it as 'yucky', then children are much less likely to play with it, whereas there is comparatively little positive effect from her reacting to the toy with positive expressions and saying it will be 'fun'.[12] The same is true for adults. We are more attuned to the negative reactions of others, especially in uncertain situations.[13]

Negativity gets its power because we remember setbacks much better than the things that go right for us. Deep in our brain exists the ancient *limbic system*, which is involved with motivation, emotions, learning and memory. Part of that system includes an almond-shaped structure called the *amygdala*, which is particularly tuned to negative experiences and acts to strengthen them as memories. The flashbulb memories of the 9/11 attacks we described in Lesson Two became more strongly encoded in the brain because the amygdala amplified the signal in the long-term memory stores. During recall, residents closest to the Twin Towers in Downtown Manhattan had stronger activation of the amygdala than those further away, in Midtown Manhattan.[14] This negativity bias operates in memory so we can learn from the bad things in the past and be prepared, should they happen again in the future.

It is not just memories that are biased towards the negative. When it comes to predicting the future, we tend to be on the lookout for negative things that might happen – especially when the signals are ambiguous. False alarms are much safer than missed threats and so a signal that is potentially dangerous is more likely to be interpreted as such rather than be treated as positive or ignored.

These negativity biases for memories and predictions must have conferred some advantage for our ancestors, otherwise, they would have disappeared over the course of evolution. The more attention we paid to threats, remembering and predicting them, the more likely we were to survive. If we heard a rustle in the bushes, it was better to think it was a lion than assume it was just the wind. Evolution selects for the best adaptations, which is why the negativity bias has been passed down the generations and is still with us today.

The world has changed, from the open African savannahs that our hunter-gatherer ancestors roamed, where real dangers lurked in the bushes, to the relative safety and comfort of modern society, where imagined dangers hide around every corner. As we saw in Lesson Two, our priority today is to be accepted and to flourish within groups, and thus the nature of threats we face has changed. Governments, authorities, rules and regulations dominate our lives, and so we are controlled by legislation and the negative consequences that might arise from failing to comply. Most of the time, we live our lives in obeyance of the rules that govern us, but that requires money. Salaries, taxes, mortgages and bills are all challenges in today's society that require individuals to have money. Without money, we are dependent on others. Poverty is aversive not only due to a lack of food, housing and other necessities of modern living, but because it creates uncertainty and insecurity that lead to chronic stress. Our place within society is determined by status, wealth and stability – issues that routinely worry us when they are uncertain. Then there are personal challenges, such as speaking in public, job interviews, exams and unrealistic expectations of perfection that are not necessarily life-threatening but can overwhelm individuals as if they are, because they engage the same mechanisms that evolved to respond to physical threat in the past.

Some of us are more trip-wired to respond negatively than others, leading us to overreact continuously. If we remain constantly vigilant and highly stressed, eventually this overreaction manifests as anxiety and impacts on our mental well-being. However, if we can recognise that these overreactions are the negativity bias at work, we can better understand our anxiety as a hangover from our days on the savannah. If you are prone to such anxiety, try the box breathing technique from Lesson Two to first regulate the body's response; and then, for the mind, use the 'detaching' happiness hack we recommended in Lesson One. Detach yourself from anxiety by saying, 'I am not an anxious person, but someone experiencing an episode of anxiety.' To that you can add, 'I am not an anxious person, but someone experiencing an emotion that allowed my ancestors to survive.' Detaching and justifying anxiety makes it less aversive and the situation more manageable.

Despite its potential faults, we must accept that a negativity bias is still a good thing to have, so long as it is applied appropriately and doesn't develop into chronic anxiety. Paying attention to negative information informs us of potentially threatening situations that we should address – whether that's harmful relationships, unemployment, illness or any of the other circumstances that make us unhappy. Like pain, unhappiness can be a necessary alarm bell which forces us to rethink our current position and make the necessary readjustments.

We should also recognise, however, our tendency to give more weight to negativity than it deserves. As we saw in Lesson Three, our affective forecasting inaccurately leads us to predict that the emotional consequences of important events will be much stronger in terms of impact and duration than they turn out to be.[15] These predictions are much stronger for negative events compared with positive ones. We think that the positive emotions from getting a job promotion will last longer and stronger than they do, but the negative consequences of being made redundant will be far more impactful by comparison. When it comes to romantic disappointments, career difficulties, political defeats, distressing news and personal rejections, affective forecasting leads us to believe that bad will be much stronger than good.

Again, this is an unfounded bias. Negative events tend not to be as bad as we imagine, whereas good ones are only marginally better than we expect. The reason for this asymmetry is that overestimating the negative consequences of events down the road steers us away from them, and that makes them more beneficial than overestimating positive outcomes. As the psychologist Roy Baumeister quipped, 'To survive, life has to win every day. Death has to win just once.'[16] So we look out for and fear the worst, which helps us to avoid the risks. However, those who are overly optimistic don't believe those future risks apply to them, and this can lead to recklessness. Clearly there needs to be a balance when it comes to optimism and prudent pessimism. But how can we make informed decisions?

If it bleeds, it leads

One of the obstacles to making informed decisions is the nature of information. First, we notice when things change, but not when they stay the same. Steady states are not informative and therefore do not require our attention. As Schopenhauer noted, 'We feel pain but not painlessness.'[17] We feel hunger but not satiation. Negative signals represent a departure from normality that require our attention, whereas positive signals do not generally need a response. If we do happen to notice positive states, then it is usually in contrast to the negative and not the other way around. We are not aware of feeling well unless our attention is drawn to it. In contrast, if we feel unwell, this immediately registers with us.

We notice unhappiness more than happiness, which is why we need to remind ourselves of the good things in life by writing gratitude letters or taking time to savour positive moments to redress the imbalance.

This focus on negative change also dominates the information that surrounds us in the media. When we hear that a war has broken out between Ukraine and Russia, that is newsworthy, but not that peace continues to be enjoyed across the rest of Europe, as it has been for the past eighty years. We read only about significant events, not the absence of events, and we rarely notice subtle gains versus obvious setbacks. 'If it bleeds, it leads' is the trope for journalism. The problem is that the constant diet of negative news that we pay attention to makes us unhappy.[18] By accentuating the negative, news outlets fuel the general impression that the world is getting more dangerous, which partly explains the pessimistic world-view we began the lesson with.

It's all too easy to blame the journalists for painting the world so darkly, but they are responding to public tastes. As consumers, we seek out negative stories. This negative focus is especially true when we feel threatened. 'Doomscrolling' was a common phenomenon during the pandemic for individuals who endlessly scrolled through the news to seek out information that was mostly negative. Not only was there a significant increase in the consumption of traditional and social media during the pandemic, but most of it was negative, with a corresponding decrease in mental well-being among those with a negative disposition.[19] Another strategy is to use sensationalist headlines that trigger strong emotional reactions, such as 'MEAT FROM CATTLE SLAUGHTERED IN "CRUEL" KOSHER

CEREMONY IS USED IN YOUR HIGH STREET BURGER'.[20] Like a road traffic accident, you cannot help but want to look, and the more negative the emotion, the stronger the response.

The take-home message is to remember these biases when you next read the news. Things are not as bad as they seem. Try to find at least one good news story. You may not be able to ignore the negative stories, but actively try to seek some balance. Adopt a more critical and sceptical view on everything you read. Remember, journalism is seldom impartial, and writers are always looking for the emotional angle to draw the reader in. Be wary of shock and sensationalist headlines – these are exactly the tactics to get audiences to read on.

Judging others

One area where we can and should make a difference in our lives is the way we judge others, because, all too often, a negativity bias creeps in to colour our opinions. Understanding how this happens is important if we are to find happiness by becoming less egocentric. When someone first meets another person, they run through a series of checks to identify and categorise them. We never get a second chance to make a first impression, especially if that first impression is negative. In fact, we don't even get as long as a second – people can form a lasting impression of others within one tenth of a second! Simply flashing a face up for 100 milliseconds triggers 'thin-slicing' attributions related to attractiveness, likeability, trustworthiness, aggressiveness and competence.[21] If you flash the face up for longer, there is comparatively little change in ratings. This speed of processing also strongly indicates unconscious or *implicit* processing, as psychologists like to say. As implicit processes operate largely under the radar of conscious awareness, they can be difficult to change. Confirmation biases operate to select subsequent information that support our initial impression. If we learn additional information about a person that should correct our first impression, we are less likely to revise a negative opinion even when we hear additional positive information. On the other hand, if we start with a good impression of someone but then hear something bad about them, we easily and quickly change our positive view of them.[22]

Even if we do take the time to learn more about others, we give much more weight to the bad versus the good that they do. We are much more likely to categorise someone who steals $5 as intensely immoral than someone who donates $5 as being intensely moral.[23] And once we have categorised someone as bad, it takes much longer to change our impression of them. For example, in a 2016 study on the tipping point for moral change, Chicago psychologists told participants about an average office worker named Barbara who was occasionally good and occasionally bad.[24] They were then told that there had been a change in Barbara's behaviour. One group were told that Barbara had started to behave consistently well whereas another group were told that she was consistently doing mean things. Participants were then asked how many weeks of this change would convince them that Barbara had really changed. On average, people thought Barbara had changed for the worse after four weeks, but it would take at least six weeks for them to consider that she had changed for the better, suggesting that we are more inclined to settle on a negative reassessment than one that is more positive. Once you reach a decision about someone, it is more difficult to revise your opinion of them.

This negativity bias impacts our capacity for forgiveness. When we are wronged, we find it harder to forgive and forget. John Gottman, an expert in marital relationships, estimates that you probably need at least five rights to make up for a wrongdoing, otherwise the relationship is doomed.[25] Gottman has studied and counselled many couples and found that it is not so much what goes right in a marriage but, rather, what goes wrong that predicts whether a relationship will survive. If you are married or in a long-term relationship, then you will have encountered many times when you said or did the wrong thing. Maybe it was a careless comment or maybe you forgot an anniversary. Of course, it depends on the nature of the transgression and what you do to repair the damage, but the negative imbalance fits with the general truism that it takes time to build a positive relationship but only an instant to destroy it.

Why are we so rigid in our thinking about others and what can we do to be fairer? We naturally and instinctively put people, especially those we don't know well, into different boxes using stereotypes. Rather than taking the time to learn more about others, we rely on shortcuts and prejudices. When we quickly misjudge others as bad, it is our negativity bias getting in the way. Moreover, we attribute their strengths and weaknesses as fundamental components of who they are rather than recognising the role of external circumstances or random luck. For example, if we observe someone driving too fast on a motorway, we are likely to regard them as a bad driver – we assume that recklessness or carelessness is their nature. However, if someone points out that we are driving too fast on a motorway, we justify our behaviour in terms of the circumstances, such as 'I was in a hurry because I was late.' We don't readily apply the same mitigating excuses to others. If we observe someone being rude then we judge them as an unkind person, but when we are rude, we defend our behaviour by saying it was justified or that this is not what we are normally like. This tendency to attribute stable features to others but transient excuses to ourselves is called the *fundamental attribution error.*[26]

We fall into the fundamental attribution error trap because we don't know or can't see the circumstances or situations that actually cause outcomes. Also, hidden causes are disturbing to us. If we see a homeless person on the street, we are more comfortable viewing them as responsible for their own predicament than understanding that they may be the victim of circumstances that could easily befall any of us. We are frightened by the possibility that we could so easily be them. We are uncomfortable with the notion of good and bad luck, and prefer to believe in a 'just deserts' world where things happen for a reason.[27] This leads us to think that people who are down and out deserve their predicament due to fundamental attributes of who they are. In contrast, we are more likely to attribute our own misfortune to external circumstances out of our control, but our successes down to our own abilities.

What is the solution to being fairer? The first thing to do is take your time with other people before making a decision about them. Don't jump to conclusions. Think about the times when you've behaved in a less than ideal way and why that was. That might help you to get better at imagining why others might behave badly. Don't rely on looks. Clothes and appearances can be deceptive. Recognise your prejudices and thin-slicing at work as well as any tendency to confirm your biases. Sometimes we don't have the opportunity, but if you do, get to know someone better. Take time to listen to and process others. Also, remember they, too, are sizing you up and may be making the wrong impression of you as well! If someone seems disadvantaged, then put yourself in their shoes. It is all too easy to distance our self from their predicament, and our tendency for just-deserts thinking means that we may be judging them unreasonably. Maybe they are down and out through no fault of their own. Taking other perspectives into account is the first step to becoming less egocentric and more allocentric. When you can imagine being in someone's situation, then you will become less critical and more generous. And as we discovered in Lesson Two, when you are kind to others, you are kind to yourself.

Learned helplessness

All these biases – to falsely attribute positive outcomes to ourselves but negative outcomes to others or to external circumstances – are largely down to the way we view the world from the egocentric perspective. We like to be the masters of our own destiny, and the notion that we are not in control is something we find psychologically upsetting. The perception of control is necessary for coping with uncertainty. Without it, we feel powerless and helpless. When individuals believe they have no control over an aversive situation, they find it more stressful and negative than it may otherwise be.[28]

Even the perception of control is beneficial. Simply believing you can change things is sufficient to boost resilience. For example, in a study where they can earn money for accepting painful shocks, it was found that individuals will tolerate greater pain if they believe they can stop the experiment at any time.[29] Pain is a warning signal but if we think we can determine the outcome, we can ignore it. Perceived control works by changing the way our brain interprets the meaning of uncertainty, making it less threatening.[30] Uncertainty makes situations more stressful because you can't predict what is going to happen. However, if you believe you have control over the situation, then you think you can stop it at any point and so this is less anxiety-inducing, which enables you to tolerate more. In contrast, taking away control or the belief that you can exert control is stressful because you never know when an aversive situation is going to end, and this uncertainty leads to despair.

Without the ability to control your own life, you experience a state of helplessness or hopelessness. One of the pioneers of positive psychology, Martin Seligman, demonstrated this in experimental animal work in the 1960s where he induced a state of *learned helplessness* in dogs by giving them an experience where they had no control over their environment.[31] In these early studies, Seligman trained dogs to associate a light with an impending mild electric shock that they could not escape. The point was to establish whether, having learned the association, dogs would be quicker to learn to avoid the consequences of the light in a new situation. Once they had learned this association, the dogs were taken to another cage, which had a small barrier across the middle separating the two halves. The half of the cage where the dog was initially placed was attached to the power supply, but if the animal simply jumped over the barrier, it could avoid the shock because the other side was safe.

The prevailing theory at the time predicted that animals who had learned that a light was a signal for an impending shock would learn to jump the barrier faster than dogs that had no experience of lights and shocks. But in fact, Seligman found the opposite pattern. Those animals that had been given uncontrollable electric shocks passively accepted their fate when the light was activated and lay down on the cage floor without trying to jump the barrier. In contrast, dogs who didn't have the experience of uncontrollable shock quickly learned to jump the barrier. This was because the dogs who had endured uncontrollable shocks had developed learned helplessness. They had learned that there was no point in trying to escape in the past, so this previous uncontrollable experience impaired their ability to adapt to new circumstances.

Seligman immediately recognised the significance of these animal studies. Maybe learned helplessness explained human despair. He went on to conduct studies with humans and found the same learned helplessness phenomenon, which led him to develop an explanation for why people become depressed and lose hope. He argued that if you had experienced uncontrollable negative life events as a child, such as poverty or a disruptive home life, this induced learned helplessness that generalised to all aspects of life when the child grew up into an adult.

When Seligman presented his theory at Oxford University, the psychiatrist John Teasdale pointed out that the problem with the original proposition was that not everyone who experiences uncontrollable adversity develops depression. Not everyone succumbs to learned helplessness. Some are more optimistic. When Seligman reviewed his own data, he discovered that there was indeed a group, around a third of animals and humans, who did not display learned helplessness, which led him to rethink his approach.[32] Who were these individuals resistant to learned helplessness and what made them different? Were there lessons to be learned from these individuals? If helplessness could be learned, was it also possible to learn to become optimistic?

Learned optimism

At the beginning of this book, we asked what makes someone more positive or negative – nature or nurture? To answer this, we can again look to identical and non-identical twin studies to estimate how much genes play a role in our disposition to be optimistic or pessimistic. Even though we usually think of optimism and pessimism as being two ends of the same spectrum, they appear to be under separate genetic influences, which fits with the way that people can compartmentalise different parts of their lives.[33] For example, we can be optimistic about our career prospects but pessimistic about our personal relationships. Twin studies indicate that the heritability of optimism is around 24 per cent whereas it is 29 per cent for pessimism. This means that although there is a genetic tendency, environment plays a predominant role for both,[34] and the home environment during childhood in particular has been found to impact on optimism. For example, a longitudinal study of individuals from infancy found that higher levels of socio-economic status at birth predicted higher levels of optimism twenty-one years later,[35] with parental input playing a critical role in their children's optimism.[36] When it comes to optimism, there is room for circumstances, learned helplessness, parental styles and the interaction of disposition.

What were these young people learning? Optimism is about moving on, looking forward and not fixating or ruminating on the past or current problems. If you recall Epictetus, he and other Stoic philosophers believed that, when it comes to happiness, it's not what happens to you, but how you respond that matters. This is where Martin Seligman and colleagues set to work – to find ways to increase optimism. What was it about optimists that made them more positive?

One thing they discovered is that optimists differ from pessimists in the way they make sense of life events, especially negative setbacks. Specifically, they identified three characteristic patterns of thinking, called *attributional styles*, that differ between optimists and pessimists.[37] The first attributional style is *pervasiveness*, which describes the extent to which we generalise, applying the features of one situation to another. For example, imagine you fail a job interview. A pessimist is more likely to infer 'I'm a failure at everything I do!', whereas the optimist is less likely to be as pervasive but, rather, ringfence the episode: 'Oh well, that's a bummer, but there are other things going well in my life.' The next attributional style is *permanence*, which reflects the extent to which the pessimist regards setbacks as everlasting – 'I am never going to get a job' – while the optimist is more likely to treat it as a temporary hiccup: 'I'll do better next time.' Finally, when it comes to attributing blame, a pessimist takes the failure as *personal* and internalises the responsibility – 'It's my fault I didn't get the job' – whereas the optimist is more likely to externalise the issue: 'It's not my fault that they couldn't see my value. They're making a big mistake in not hiring me.' In this situation, the optimist is deflecting the blame onto others.

Using this information about attributional style, Seligman developed a resilience programme he calls the 'ABCDE' technique, which stands for Adversity, Belief, Consequence, Dispute and Energise.[38] The aim of the programme is to teach you to be more optimistic when facing setbacks. ABC is the first part of the exercise, where you note down the nature of the 'adversity' in as much detail as possible – what you 'believe' happened and the 'consequences'. The point is to provide as much information to address as possible. Returning to the job interview example, the ABC would be that you failed to get a job (adversity) because you think that you gave a bad interview (belief) and this will mean that you will never get a job (consequence). Once you have documented this information in the ABC phase, you then go on the offensive in the DE part to 'dispute' or challenge beliefs and consequences, or at least find alternative, less negative interpretations.

The best way to dispute is to adopt a more optimistic attributional style, reinterpreting the ABC evidence by being less pervasive, permanent and personal. One way to think about this is from the distanced self-perspective. If you are someone who internalises the responsibility for a negative outcome, cannot see that the problem is only temporary and that there are other things going on in your life, you are falling foul of the overly egocentric self. Optimists ignore or diminish personal failings by turning their attention elsewhere or moving on to other things, while pessimists extrapolate negativity to all aspects of their lives. By adopting a more allocentric perspective, you avoid the negative attributional style of the pessimist.

Armed with an optimistic attributional style, it is possible to dispute, dismiss, undermine or reinterpret any setback to frame it in a more positive light. Take a step back and imagine that you are a lawyer or barrister defending yourself as a client. For every dark cloud, there is always a silver lining. In the failed job interview example, dispute that you gave a bad interview. Tell yourself that you gave a good interview but there was probably an internal candidate, or the interviewers did not know what they were looking for. Challenge the idea that it was anything to do with you. Congratulate yourself on getting to the interview stage and imagine all the hundreds of applicants that did not even get shortlisted.

Finally, once you have reinterpreted the setback in a more positive way, this should allow you to become more 'energised' – the final component of the ABCDE technique. Take pride in the way that you have dealt with your problem, with the knowledge that you can take back control of your negative thoughts and pessimism. Look towards a positive future, more energised by your learned optimism. Maybe that job wasn't the right job for you and you dodged a bullet. This means that you are free to apply for an even better job that comes along.

Another way to become more optimistic is to force yourself to think of a future that is even better than you currently imagine. Think of the best possible version of yourself in the future. Invest in a journal to write down your thoughts for ten minutes each day. Imagine that everything is better than you'd expected. You can take one aspect of your life and address it each week to spread the exercise out. Partner: imagine the best possible partner. Who would they be? What are they like? Family: imagine the best family life you could have. What would it be like? Career: imagine that you have achieved the ideal job. What is it and what provides the most satisfaction? Friends: how many friends would you like and how would you spend time with them? What's the best possible social life you could have? Whatever aspect of yourself you consider important, imagine the best possible version of it in the future. Be as creative and imaginative as possible. Don't hold back. Studies have shown that when you are forced to imagine the best possible future, this leaves you feeling more optimistic.[39]

Optimism and health

We said at the beginning of this lesson that optimists are healthier and live longer. Large epidemiological studies consistently show that individuals who are most pessimistic have more health problems and die on average around eight to ten years earlier than the most optimistic.[40] Pessimists succumb more easily to the major killers of cardiovascular disease, respiratory problems and cancer. One major contributing factor is chronic stress. We have already flagged the fight-flight response as a potential mechanism related to stress in Lesson Two. The link between these diseases and the role of chronic stress on the body's immune and inflammatory response systems to combat disease and infection is well established. Stress is compounded by perceived threat and uncertainty about the future. As optimists view the future more positively, this outlook enables them to adopt healthier lifestyles aided by greater social support.

It is important to clarify that optimism is not the same as hope. Hope is an emotional state most closely related to wishing for important – but less likely – outcomes that are more out of our control.[41] Optimists go further in that they *believe* outcomes will be better and so work harder, longer and persevere when pessimists give up. This has implications for leading healthier lifestyles and adhering to health recommendations to prevent disease progression.[42] A second advantage is the optimistic mindset. Optimists are resilient. They persist in overcoming stressors, which may test the body's physiological system to the extreme but, in the end, is more likely to lead to eventual resolution of the stressor. In contrast, pessimists give up more readily, but even then the stressors are not resolved as the problem is not perceived as going away.[43] This leads to chronic stress and a negative impact on our immune function and our reaction to chronic stress, as noted in Lesson Two. A third explanation is related to social support and loneliness. Optimists are perceived as more likeable, attractive and friendly compared to pessimists. They have larger social networks and greater social support.[44] In later life, optimism predicts greater defence against loneliness and all the negative implications that being isolated can have for one's health.[45]

Overall, optimists are less likely to give up in the face of health challenges. They are also more likely to reframe situations as challenges rather than threats, and engage in healthier practices to ensure better futures. They have goals and the confidence to achieve them, which bolsters their ability to combat disease.

But a word of caution. Optimism might be a healthier frame of mind and the spur that drives one on to achieve goals, but unrealistic optimism can lead to recklessness. If you are some-one with attributional styles that lead you to regard failures as isolated, temporary and not your fault, then you may not learn from your mistakes. If we don't learn from our mistakes, then we are likely to repeat the same errors. If you don't think health risks apply to you, then you may lead an unhealthy lifestyle. We should seek to be more optimistic, but we must also temper this positive mindset with a degree of realism.

I advise combining positive outlooks with reasonable fore-sight and planning. One technique that has proven successful is *mental contrasting*, which combines exercises for motivation, planning and execution.[46] It is called contrasting because you are expected to mentalise achieving the desired outcome con-trasted with the challenges that stand in the way. First, in order to strive for goals, one has to imagine that these are achievable. As many sports psychologists advocate, visualising or imag-ing achieving a goal stimulates the motivation to pursue that objective. The more specific the target the better, as this adds tangible performance indicators to determine whether progress towards the goal is being achieved. However, just wishing for a future goal is not enough. That would be hope, which is not a good strategy for success. As the psychologist Gabrielle Oettingen has argued, wishful thinking leads to inertia.[47] You need to also think about future obstacles and how you might overcome them.

Oettingen has developed a technique called WOOP that uses mental contrasting to achieve goals.[48] WOOP stands for Wish, Outcome, Obstacles, Plan. Begin by identifying what you 'wish' for in as much detail as possible. Don't be vague – 'I want to lose weight' – but, rather, set specific gaols – 'I want to lose

10lbs'. Specific goals are more tangible and achievable. They provide a measurable yardstick for progress. Next, imagine the 'outcome' of losing 10lbs. Visualise standing on the scales and how good you will feel when you see you have lost that weight. Wish and outcome are necessary to motivate you to change your lifestyle. However, you need a strategy. What are the 'obstacles'? Perhaps: 'I don't have time to prepare my own fresh food. Buying processed food is easier.' Consider these obstacles and what plans you can implement to overcome them – 'Don't buy cakes. Put temptation out of sight. Eat more fresh fruit and vegetables. Learn to cook simple nutritious meals', etc.

Following a mental contrasting strategy like WOOP is much more likely to work than simply wanting to change. In one study of over 10,000 German women wishing to eat more fresh fruit and vegetables, two groups were educated about the benefits of switching to a healthier diet, while one group was also taught the WOOP technique.[49] For positive visualisation, they were told to imagine how great the outcome would be if they actually ate more fresh fruit and vegetables. But what are the obstacles? Maybe finding a regular supply of fresh produce is challenging. Or maybe you enjoy a weekly pizza night. Forewarned by the potential obstacles, they could make contingency plans – 'In that case, I will need to join a cooperative food group or sign up to a home delivery service that specialises in fresh produce and delivers it every week. I will limit my pizza night to once every two weeks for the first two months and then once a month.' The other group just went about their normal routines without the contingency planning.

Initially there was no difference between the two groups in terms of healthy eating. By four months, however, the groups were beginning to diverge, with the normal routine group eating less fresh produce; two years into the study, they had returned to their original eating habits. The WOOP group, meanwhile, had maintained healthier eating. Being optimistic is all well and good, but one also has to take action to live healthier.

In this lesson we have learned that different facets of our lives generate different expectations for the future, and although we each have dispositions to think both optimistically and pessimistically, we can all learn to become more positive. We reviewed the benefits of thinking positively and the challenges of negative biases. Both are valuable, so long as they are not taken to the extreme. It is useful to pay attention to warning signals but negativity must not come to dominate our thinking. It is better to be optimistic for our health and happiness but we should also exercise a degree of caution to avoid recklessness. Recognising attributional styles and thinking less egocentrically are solutions to becoming more optimistic. Another is to imagine a better future for ourselves and planning the necessary actions to get there. In the next lesson we highlight a major challenge to becoming happier, which is what happens to our minds when we are inactive or not actively engaged in some task or other. It's a time when our minds are not focused and when negativity biases can dominate our thoughts. However, armed with the strategies we've learned in this lesson, we will be able to take back control of our attention.

Happiness exercises

Imagine the best possible future for yourself. Detach from your current situation and imagine your ideal situation in five years' time. Write down what that might be like.

Remember that news tends to be negative. Limit the amount of news you consume. Check the amount of time on your phone that is spent on social media or news apps and try to reduce it. Remember that our attention is automatically drawn to the negative.

Persevere at forgiveness. The next time you do something wrong to someone you care about, remember that it will require many more attempts to repair the damage. Persevere in your efforts rather than regarding the other person as unreasonable. Try to be both more forgiving and willing to make amends.

Practise learned optimism. If you experience a setback that leaves you upset, try the ABCDE technique to reframe the situation more positively.

Use the WOOP mental contrasting technique to achieve goals. Make positive plans for the future and balance these with pragmatic steps to ensure that change happens.

LESSON FIVE

Control Your Attention

Every night, our dreams open a window into our unconscious mind with a typical flurry of unfettered thoughts and images. One fleeting idea triggers another without the need for any logic. This chaos is what makes dreams so marvellous, terrifying or dumbfounding – visions that escape reality. There is one aspect of dreaming that is constant, however. You may not remember the dream you had last night, but if you can, I bet my bottom dollar that you were in it. Irrespective of whether the dream was pleasant, unpleasant or one of those bizarre fantasies where nothing makes sense, you were still the main character in your own midnight show. It may seem obvious, but it is worth pointing out that we don't dream of events that do not involve us. Even if the dream involves observing others or events, we are still the ones doing the observing. It is impossible to imagine what a dream would be without the observing self.

This egocentric self who occupies our dreams is also present for most of our waking mental life. During the waking day, we spend a considerable amount of time dreaming, especially when we are not fully focused on a task. This kind of dreaming is more akin to mind-wandering than the chaotic, vivid, visual imagery of the night-time picture show. While mind-wandering can involve pleasant recollections or wishful hopes for the future, as we will discover, it often leads us to focus on negative thoughts and worries that we can't seem to resolve.

In this lesson, I want to focus on our preoccupation with ourselves or our problems when our mind is left to wander. We will consider how awareness needs to be focused when we work on tasks that require our concentration, but also how that awareness easily strays towards self-focus and rumination when our attention is not captured. When we are not task-occupied, we spend our time travelling into our imagination.

We will explore how humans spend their time imagining possible futures. Those of us who are anxious or unhappy may worry constantly about unresolved problems. Some of the time, this manifests as an internal monologue, a constant voice in our minds about how problematic our lives are and how inadequate we are in comparison to others. We ruminate about the past or worry about problems that might arise in the future. We blow every minor problem out of proportion and, in doing so, constantly cripple our own efforts to achieve happiness. When we are unhappy, we are cursed to keep turning our thoughts inwards towards our inadequacies. We can be optimistic when we are asked to consider our distant futures, as we noted in the last lesson, but if there is an issue looming on the near horizon that needs fixing, we tend to be more negative.

No matter how much you try to stay focused, your mind

will wander. We talk about having a train of thought as if ideas are like carriages that follow one another, but as the philosopher William James pointed out, our subjective experience of consciousness is more fluid.[1] It is the dynamic nature of consciousness that it will ebb, flow and drift and then at other times wiggle and fidget like an impatient toddler. Even as you read this, your mind will at times drift elsewhere. You are engaged in a constant battle with everything that competes to draw your attention. You might imagine that in a bland situation with nothing to draw our attention, we might experience less mind-wandering, but in fact the opposite happens.[2] You know it yourself. Whenever we get bored, our minds wander. And when that happens, negative thoughts easily intrude into our stream of consciousness, impacting our happiness.

Why is mind-wandering so common and what is its purpose? Why do we ruminate? After all, brain activity is metabolically expensive, and we would not have evolved mind-wandering unless it served some function. The answers lie in the way our minds imagine ourselves in past, current and future scenarios by activation of circuitry in the brain that provides the platform for us to think about ourselves and the problems we face. Once we become aware of our problems, we focus on them in an attempt to solve them, and therein lies the source of our worry and unhappiness. If we have a tendency to regard our life as problematic, as we clearly do with the various negativity biases that we examined in the last lesson, then left to our devices we are in danger of becoming preoccupied with negative thoughts. Here we will learn why this happens, and what we can do to quieten our worrisome mind when it strays into negative thinking. Finally, we will consider and practise techniques to distance our egocentric self from excessive worrying so that we may feel calmer and happier.

Time travellers

As adults, many of us find staying in the present moment quite challenging if we are not focused on a task, due to our involuntary tendency towards mind-wandering when we're bored.[3] Children also mind-wander when bored, but unlike adults they do not typically have a bias to mentally time-travel to the past or the future. They just get distracted easily by what is currently going on. In fact, thinking about the past and future is quite difficult for most young children.[4] When asked what they did 'yesterday' and what they will do 'tomorrow', two thirds of three-year-olds were unable to do so.[5] When asked to think about the past and future, children could do this from five to six years of age, but not spontaneously – only in response to prompts from the adult interviewer.[6] In one study, of spontaneous mental time-travel, children aged six to seven and nine to ten years, plus adolescents and adults, were asked to draw a picture and whenever a 'ding' went off on the computer, they were to report whatever was on their mind and whether it was in the past, present or future. Although everyone's minds were wandering on about a third of the times they were probed, only the adults reported a bias to be thinking mostly about the future.[7]

Young children may not think so much about the future because they lack the experience and knowledge to imagine that future, but they can dream of being older; especially as they become more aware of the freedoms enjoyed by adults.

'When I grow up ...' is a common phrase used by children to indicate the aspiration for the privileges of adulthood. But just as Tom Hanks's man-child character Josh Baskin discovers in the 1988 fantasy movie *Big*, where a twelve-year-old is magically transformed into an adult overnight, adulthood comes with much anxiety and worry.

With age, we spend increasing amounts of time thinking about the past and future. Much of the effort we expend today is in the service of achieving happiness later down the road. As noted by the Greek philosopher Aristotle, most of our activities and thoughts are in service of the hedonic principle to seek happiness as an end goal. Education, exams, training, jobs, relationships are all in the service of making provision for the future, but mental life was not always so future-focused. In our distant past as hunter-gatherers, we lived mostly on a day-to-day basis with little provision and planning for the long term. Like many other animals, we simply followed the migration of herds or returned to familiar patches where fruits and berries could be expected to ripen at different times of the year. Existence was very much subsistence-living, tied to changing natural patterns around us. With the invention of farming around 12,000 years ago, we were able to take control over nature and the seasons. We could artificially change the natural patterns to our benefit, but this required us to settle down and make longer-term plans. We began to rear animals, plant crops and establish communities where planning became paramount to survival. These communities could not simply uproot and move to new hunting grounds but had to lay down foundations for the long-term – crops and herds had to be nurtured and tended. Sowing and harvesting had to be planned.

Animal enclosures had to be constructed and maintained. Successful farming required thinking about the future.

Making plans was possible because the brain evolved as a prediction engine. We use past experiences and information about our current state to predict the future, which allows us to increase the odds of desired outcomes while avoiding or bracing ourselves for future adversity. However, waiting for those outcomes is stressful due to uncertainty and unpredictability. As explored in previous lessons, when we are forced to wait for an uncertain outcome we experience a loss of control and enter a heightened state of preparation for the fight flight response, which, as we have already seen, impacts negatively on health. If we can do something about our uncertain circumstances by enacting a plan of action, this produces coping behaviour, a psychologically more resilient state of mind than hopelessness, worries or fears for the future.

Even though very few of us today farm for our survival, we all still have plenty to worry about when it comes to predicting the future. Concerns around our jobs, cost of living, climate change, homelessness, interest rates, redundancy, illness, bills, conflicts and relationships trigger our worrisome mind and all the associated coping strategies to regain control. It's enough to make you want to be an egocentric child again, living in the moment.

Idle thoughts

Before the modern era, the toil of daily lives for most people was unrelenting and laborious. Prior to industrialisation, looking after yourself and your family took up a large part of the waking day as there were none of the conveniences of modern life. Food preparation and domestic duties left little time for other pastimes. Hunting, gathering, tending crops, ploughing and sowing, washing and repairing clothes, looking after livestock and maintaining a homestead required everyone to contribute, including the children. In short, we were preoccupied with just surviving. Life revolved around the rise and setting of the sun as there was little that could be done in the dark, so people went to bed early and awoke with sunrise to begin the day's work.

Most of us worked longer and physically harder, until technological developments began to make labouring easier. The wheel, the plough, fertilisers and financial commerce are just some of the human inventions that enabled the agricultural revolution. Machines started to make our lives easier. Farming increased productivity and capitalism provided the constant incentive to keep working and expand our efforts beyond self-sufficiency. In the West, workers moved into the factories and toiled long shifts to fuel the industrial revolution. By the nineteenth century, however, labour-saving technological advances also created a 'leisure revolution' where common workers had more free time.[8] Artificial lighting lengthened the day, providing more hours to be active rather than going to bed. There had always been time set aside for contemplation, especially religious devotion, but this was nothing in comparison to the time that was now available. In the West, the average working week declined from sixty-to-seventy hours per week in 1870, to the current thirty-to-forty hours per week. We also have more holidays than we did 150 years ago.[9]

When we are not working for an income, the rest of the

time is spent on various chores including household maintenance, food preparation, eating, travel and, finally, leisure. Today, we should have more spare time on our hands than ever before, thanks to technological advances. And yet, most of us complain that we are still too busy. How often have you asked someone how things are going, and they answer, 'Busy'? We are busy, but not necessarily productive. In one influential study[10] by psychologists Matt Killingsworth and Dan Gilbert, over 15,000 participants were randomly contacted during the waking day via an app on their iPhone and asked a series of questions including:

'What are you doing now?'

'Are you thinking about something other than what you're currently doing?'

'How do you feel on a scale of very bad to very good?'

They were also asked whether their current thoughts were pleasant, neutral or negative.

Nearly half of the time, participants were thinking about something other than what they were doing. Mind-wandering was most frequent during preening activities, such as showering or brushing teeth, at around 65 per cent of responders, but it also happened around 50 per cent of the time that they were supposed to be focused on work. The one activity where people were not mind-wandering as much was during sex, with only 10 per cent of reports (arguably still too many). But it does beg the question, 'Who responds to a survey during or immediately after sex?'

This and other similar sampling studies have also shown

that mind-wandering takes up a large part of the waking day.[11] Although people were more likely to wander to pleasant topics (42.5 per cent of samples) compared to unpleasant topics (26.5 per cent of samples) or neutral topics (31 per cent of samples), they were no happier thinking about pleasant topics compared to when they were not mind-wandering. In contrast, when they were mind-wandering about unpleasant or neutral topics, they were considerably unhappier compared to when their minds had not wandered. This finding led Killingsworth and Gilbert to conclude, 'A wandering mind is an unhappy mind.' This study supports the negativity bias we identified in the last lesson when we are not task-focused. Is this because people's minds wander when they are experiencing some unhappiness – searching for something better? This interpretation would be consistent with research showing that inducing a negative mood leads to increased mind-wandering in the laboratory.[12] However, in real life the answer appears to be the other way round. When Killingsworth and Gilbert looked at instances when mind-wandering and happiness happened in quick succession in their random sampling study, they found that the mind-wandering was more likely to precede the bout of unhappiness rather than follow it. In other words, we become unhappy *after* our minds start to wander.

When our minds wander, a circuit in our brain known as the *default mode network* kicks into action.[13] This circuitry was first discovered during the early days of brain-imaging, when researchers measured how much more active different parts of the brain became during specific tasks. It was assumed that different parts of the brain were specialised for specific mental functions. To measure these, participants undertook various tasks that were believed to tap into these functions, to see whether there was increased blood flow to these specific regions as they worked harder to solve the task. To calculate the change in blood flow, researchers compared activity during the task with a resting period, when presumably there was no mental effort being expended on the task. During these resting periods, participants were told not to think of anything. What they discovered, and what has since been found many times over in other studies, is that rather than becoming inactive during a period of rest or when the participant is told not to think about anything, a network of brain regions involving the *medial prefrontal cortex, the posterior cingulate* and the *angular gyrus* kicks into action. It was named the default mode network (DMN) because it was the default resting state of the brain when not otherwise engaged in tasks.

The DMN and, in particular, the medial prefrontal cortex (mPFC), is where we store neural representations of ourselves. If we are asked to think about ourselves, or remember some autobiographical memory, our mPFC is activated.[14] What is remarkable is that the mPFC is active not only when we are thinking about ourselves but also about others.[15] When our mind wanders, we are thinking about ourselves and our relation to others, and this tends towards unhappiness, possibly as a result of comparison or competition, as described in Lesson Three.

Since its discovery, the DMN has been the source of much research due to its role in happiness. Individuals with major depression show increased functional connectivity in the DMN, which is associated with excessive negative rumination about their lives.[16] Some of us spend an inordinate amount of time worrying, as captured in the Mark Twain witticism 'My life has been filled with many tragedies, most of which never occurred.' The structure and function of the DMN is also altered in people who are isolated, with a 'lonelier' neural self-representation, which distorts the internal neural representation of others.[17] We are making ourselves miserable through overactivation of the DMN, but there are ways to combat a wandering mind, especially when it strays towards the negative.

Take in the great outdoors

The number of ramblers, hillwalkers, hikers and visitors to national and country parks indicate that many of us like to spend time wandering around in nature. Humans have a positive affiliation towards nature as a legacy of our evolutionary history, known as the *biophilia hypothesis*.[18] The word 'biophilia' comes from the Greek for life ('bio') and love ('philia').

Most of us prefer to be in natural environments because the modern architectural world is one that does not fit with a brain that evolved on the African savannahs. A random-sampling study of 20,000 responders (using the same smartphone technique described earlier) asked people how happy they were and then cross-referenced the answer with their GPS location. Across the UK towns, cities and countryside, people were significantly and substantially happier outdoors in all green or natural habitat types than they were in urban environments.[19] Contact with nature is also linked to a greater sense of connectedness, which is important for mental well-being, as we will explore in more detail in Lesson Six.[20] A recent meta-analysis of forty-nine studies reported that exposure to natural environments had the same medium to large effect on increasing positive mood as it did on decreasing negative mood.[21] Why is nature so beneficial to mental well-being?[22]

Being in nature causes specific changes to two related brain mechanisms, one to do with our reaction to stress and the other related to the mind-wandering. As noted earlier, stress activates our physiological threat-response systems, including increased heart rate and blood pressure, and the release of the stress hormone cortisol, but these are reduced when we are in natural environments such as forests.[23] Compared with urban environments, being in nature seems to bolster our ability to recover from stressful experiences by activating the parasympathetic system to counter the fight-or-flight reaction related to fear.[24] Fear activates the amygdala even when we are not even explicitly aware there is a threat.[25] We can experience an implicit sense of foreboding and be constantly on edge as our brains are in alert mode looking out for potential dangers. Living in a large city increases this wariness. Over time, this impacts the way we cope with threat. In one prominent brain-imaging study, three groups of German participants – city dwellers, those with both urban and rural experience, and those living in the countryside – were put under stressful conditions where they had to solve arithmetic problems under the disapproving feedback of examiners.[26] Only those who were currently living in large urban cities exhibited increased amygdala activity, relative to the other groups. Those who had been raised in a rural setting but now lived in the city showed activation in a network that regulated the amygdala, negative emotions and reactions to stress, indicating that their early upbringing in the countryside had provided them with resilience. However, all is not lost for city dwellers as in a study involving residents of Berlin, just one hour walking in nature was shown to deactivate the amygdala.[27] For optimal exposure, one large-scale study of nearly 20,000 adults found that two hours in natural spaces per week, either all at once or spread out, is all you need for significantly better self-reports of health and well-being.[28] Any longer than two hours had little additional benefit. However, it is worth noting that walking in nature only really benefits those who are motivated in the first place; forcing someone to visit the countryside is ineffectual and may even be counterproductive.[29]

In addition to deactivating the amygdala, walking in nature has also been shown to deactivate a second neural mechanism related to happiness: the mPFC region of the DMN.[30] This deactivation is stronger in nature walks compared to urban walks and associated with less mind-wandering.[31] Natural environments restore our powers of focused attention, as shown by participants' enhanced performance on lab-based tasks that tap into the executive functions of the brain's frontal lobes following a period in nature.[32] As city dwellers, our minds wander because we are so familiar with our urban environments. Have you ever noticed on your daily commute how often you have forgotten most of the journey? Mind-wandering is particularly common during monotonous motorway driving, where drivers reported being unaware up to 70 per cent of the time.[33] The routine nature of over-learned journeys and tasks, particularly in familiar environments, lures us to internal distraction as our minds go off on their own.

If you do find yourself ruminating while walking in an

urban environment, then try to be more aware of your sur-roundings. Even in the city, this will help with combating negative thoughts. Mindfulness is the practice of deliberately selecting and reinvigorating our attention on aspects of our environment that we have become accustomed to. You could focus on the placement of your feet as you walk but I prefer to pay attention to the environment by looking up, above eye level, to discover unique features in the buildings that I have not noticed before. Or take a break from listening to music on your smartphone or insulating yourself from the sounds of the city as most commuters do, and notice how the soundscapes change as you move about. Try taking a different route home or explore somewhere you haven't been before. One reason we enjoy visiting other cultures in other cities is the novel sights and sounds, but new experiences are to be found at or close to home if only we pay attention to them.

Attentional spotlights

Our minds wander when our attention is drawn away from a task, because our brains can only process a finite amount of information arising from internal and external sources. We can sometimes control our attention through voluntary effort; for example, when we are trying to hear what someone is saying in a noisy room – we can concentrate on their words by actively trying to ignore the other distracting sounds. But generally, attention is like an adjustable spotlight that can have a focused or diffuse beam (Fig. 5.1).

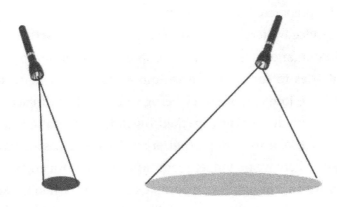

Fig. 5.1: Attention as a beam of light that can be focused or diffuse.

When the beam is focused, there is high resolution to pick out any detail. When the beam is broad, there is less resolution but a wider range that you can attend to. (Anything falling outside the beams goes unnoticed.) When attention is widely distributed, however, it can be easily distracted. There is only one attentional spotlight, and although we may think we can pay equal attention to more than one thing at a time, such multitasking does not actually happen. We just think we can multitask because we can move the spotlight quickly.

For most of the time, the stream of consciousness we each experience usually has this quality of user-control – of our self being in charge of the direction of thought that we take: 'That's an interesting idea – I think I will dwell on that for a moment.' However, sometimes we can feel overwhelmed by a situation that demands our attention; I remember how stressed I became in my first job as I attempted to serve customers demanding their drinks in a crowded bar. (Over time I learned the job and was better prepared to cope, but I have always retained a sympathy for novice waiters and bar staff who are clearly overwhelmed.)

In demanding situations, the spotlight beam jumps around as it tries to focus on the various competing demands. And when we lose that sense of being in control, it can seem as if our minds have been hijacked by some external agent. This creates the unnerving experience, in moments of extreme stress, where we no longer seem capable of organising and controlling our thoughts. In a complex situation, when faced with alternatives that require careful consideration, this can lead to anxiety. For example, driving around an unfamiliar city where there are a multitude of potential signs and different routes to consider is more stressful than the usual familiar journey one makes where the options are narrowed. Being overwhelmed with alternatives explains the tyranny of choices we encountered in Lesson Three, where having more choices led to greater indecision and unhappiness.

Then there are situations where we are automatically drawn to distracting or intrusive thoughts that disrupt our search for solutions. In a busy day, when there are many things competing for our attention, to progress with our constructive thinking we must effortfully ignore distractions. The problem with ignoring or inhibiting an unwanted thought or idea is that this creates a rebound effect called *ironic thought suppression*, which is the bane of rumination and negative thinking.[34] The thought is 'ironic' because however much you want to avoid it, it becomes the most prominent in your mind. Even if you successfully suppress the thought, it later comes back stronger – often when you are least expecting it.

To demonstrate ironic thought suppression, I want you to try the next example of mind control. First, for one minute, you're going to examine the contents of your mind. This is called *introspection* – where you turn your attentional spotlight inwardly and inspect the nature of your own thoughts. But before you start, you need to know there is one rule: you can have any thoughts you wish, but with one exception – you must not think about a white polar bear. Remember, anything but the white bear. Try it now.

If you are like most people given this task, then within about thirty seconds of being told not to think about the white bear, it is the very thought that pops into your mind.[35]

We are often tormented by unwanted thoughts that we try to ignore. When we lie awake at night, unable to sleep, we toss and turn trying not to think about the very things that are keeping us awake. Psychologist Dan Wegner explains that ironic thoughts are a consequence of trying to control our intrusive thoughts. The very act of trying to suppress an unwanted thought strengthens its representation in the mind because it has fallen under the spotlight beam of attention. If you then try to ignore this thought, you engage in the monitoring of your stream of thoughts just to check that it has not reappeared, which in turn increases the likelihood that it will enter your awareness again.

In Wegner's view, the term mind-wandering is inaccurate because it suggests a lackadaisical meander through the contents of our minds rather than a constant battle. As he puts it, 'The mind wanders, not just away from where we aim it, but also toward what we forbid it to explore.'[36] Intrusive thoughts disrupt our concentration and pull us to darker places, and the more we try to ignore them, the stronger they pull. What can we do to control this disobedient imp of a mind?

Mindfulness meditation

Let's see if we can put mental self-examination to good use. If you suffer from intrusive negative thoughts, then meditation may be a solution to your problem. Meditation has become a staple ingredient of well-being programmes due to its benefits in alleviating psychological stress.[37] There are different forms of meditation, but they all involve introspection and mind control. Introspection is when you turn your attention inwards to the contents of your mind. Mind control refers to directing the attentional spotlight. One way to achieve mind control is to deliberately and effortfully direct attention to a source other than the subject of your thoughts. This could be sensory experiences such as the feelings in your body, the nature of your breathing or the distant sounds in your environment. Some meditations involve chanting or reciting a mantra – a phrase or sound that occupies the attentional resources of the mind. As there is only one spotlight, you cannot simultaneously be focused on two thoughts at once. If you can control where your spotlight of attention is directed, this stops intrusive thoughts from hijacking your mind.

One technique combines the spotlight focus of attention with the calming effects of meditation. Known as *mindfulness meditation,* it uses directed attention to focus on the present moment. As we noted earlier, you can take mindful walks in nature to combat mind-wandering, where you focus on features you may have not noticed before. When combined with meditation, mindfulness focuses attention on the here and now, in combination with relaxation and deep breathing to achieve calm. Given the impish nature of intruding thoughts, especially those which are threatening or negative, a guided mindfulness meditation is probably the easiest way to achieve mind control. With guided meditation, you listen and respond to the instructions of a guide, who tells you when and where to direct your attention. For example, a guided meditation could work with the following commands: 'Close your eyes and focus on your breath ... Now deliberately move your attentional spotlight around your body, starting with the soles of your feet and then gradually moving slowly up your body like a scanner ... If unwanted thoughts come to mind, don't try to stop thinking about them ... Recognise them and acknowledge them ... Don't judge or consider, just notice them ... Imagine them as clouds and then visualise them as they float away ... Watch them disappear into the distance ... Now return your focus onto your breathing.' The aim is to gently guide our attention back to breathing or other sensory experiences instead of focusing on thoughts.

Guided meditation works because the instructions are from an external source, and so it is easier to disengage from our own mental perspective when directed to do so. It has been shown in attention research that moving our spotlight in response to an external command is more effective than trying to initiate the movement ourselves.[38] These external commands wrench control away from the negative thoughts. Also, the instruction to recognise, acknowledge and then ignore thoughts prevents the ironic suppression that intrusive thoughts can generate if we actively try to suppress them. In the original white bear studies, those participants who had put in effort to suppress thoughts then experienced an ironic backlash after the challenge, becoming particularly absorbed by thoughts of the polar creature.[39] Like a spring, the more effort you put in to squash it, the stronger it bounces back.

Meditation has increased in popularity in recent years, both among the public and the research community interested in its health benefits, with guided meditation apps such as Headspace (which has 70 million users) being particularly successful. While there are many studies that claim long-term benefits of meditation on a variety of well-being measures, from mental health to physical, many are flawed and biased. It is difficult to conduct stringent clinical evaluations of meditation because such studies require controlled conditions where subjects are unaware or 'blinded' to the intervention they are receiving, which is problematic given that the practice is so widespread and well known. The problem with unblinded studies is that people may report increased benefits because they expect them, which is known as the *placebo effect*. If we believe some intervention will do us good, it generally tends to do so.

There are, however, unquestionable immediate benefits of relaxation, controlled breathing and thought-regulation exercises, typical of meditation, that can be measured in real time. As we learned in Lesson One, controlled deep breathing activates the parasympathetic system to counter the fight-or-flight response, which, if left unchecked, leads to chronic stress and all the negative complications that can bring. This effect can be measured using psychophysiological changes to the respiratory, cardiovascular, cardiorespiratory and autonomic nervous systems.[40] There are also studies that show long-term changes in brain activity as a result of meditation, which cannot be dismissed as mere placebo or user expectations. Specifically, activity in the default mode network (DMN) that we discussed in relation to self and other representation and mind-wandering is dampened down by meditation. One of the most impressive is a study of novice and experienced meditators who'd had over 10,000 hours of meditation practice.[41] Brain-imaging revealed that, in comparison to the novices, experienced meditators exhibited overall reduced activation of the DMN, including reduced distractibility and mind-wandering. The experienced meditators demonstrated greater control over their minds as activation of their DMN was suppressed.

Find your flow

Before you worry about drifting off and becoming bedevilled by intrusive negative thoughts, it should be noted that not all mind-wandering is unpleasant. Indeed, most of the time our minds wander towards pleasant topics, but as noted earlier, these thoughts don't make us any happier than when we are task focused. As the attentional spotlight waxes and wanes, your mind moves through an emotional scale, spending much of the time sitting mostly in the neutral zone. At other times we take a flight of fancy that can be pleasant and productive, especially when we take control.[42] Under these circumstances, this intentional mind-wandering is where we tune out from a current task to deliberately turn our attention to something else of interest. The Israeli neuroscientist Moshe Bar believes that such mind-wandering enables us to look for associations between the various thoughts we may have.[43] It's a bit like the mental housekeeping that takes place during our nightly dreaming, but a lot less surreal. This search for associations can sometimes be fruitful, when a new insight takes place or when an idea is incubated. You can run simulations in your mind where you can imagine how things might turn out. One of the best ways to achieve positive mind-wandering is during creative acts that tap into our skill sets. Musicians, artists, writers can all experience episodes of positive mind-wandering when they look for new ideas and associations to form.

In everyday life, we strive to find positive experiences when we achieve a balance between what we think, feel and do. These goals are not always aligned. We may want to work but not enjoy the activity. It is very hard to be motivated and productive when you actively dislike what you are doing. If, on the other hand, you can find an activity that occupies your mind and makes you feel good, then there is a good chance that you will enter a state of *flow*.[44] 'Flow' was coined by the late Mihaly Csikszentmihalyi to capture those moments of alignment when what we do, think and feel are on the same page.

The best examples that capture the notion of flow are activities that require skill and concentration and generate contentment. Athletes, artists, musicians and hobbyists can all experience serene moments of flow when time seems to slip away, external pressures recede and there is reduced sense of the egocentric self. It should be an activity that taxes your ability without overwhelming it. The equation for achieving flow is illustrated by the differing relationships between levels of challenge and skill (Fig. 5.2). Flow occurs when high challenges match our skills.

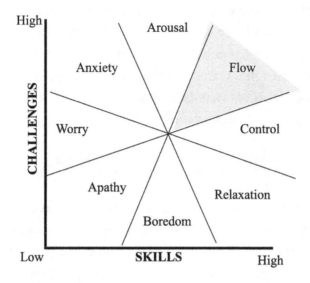

Fig. 5.2: The relationship between skill and challenge predicts the
psychological reaction. When both skill and challenge are high,
an optimal state of 'flow' can be achieved.
(Adapted from Csikszentmihalyi, 1990)

If there is a mismatch, then this leads to different emotional
outcomes. For example, if an activity requires little skill or
challenge, this leads to apathy. If it represents a major challenge and you are low in skill to address the problem, this
generates anxiety. If you are overly skilled and the challenge
is minor, then this generates relaxation but not flow.

Experiences that generate flow occur when there is an optimal relationship between challenge and skill. For example,
skiing is an activity that has varying levels of skill and challenge for novices through to experts, but regularly generates
reports of flow. Skiers can choose different paths down the

mountain, from the very easy and gentle slopes (green runs) to the most difficult steep descents (black diamond runs). If you are an expert skier, you will seek out the black diamond runs because this matches your skill level, whereas a novice can stick to the green runs. By matching challenge to skill, both levels of skier will be able to find flow.

Inner voices

Although the notion of optimal challenges is often attributed to flow and positive mental well-being, it is very similar to an older concept from child psychology called the *zone of proximal development*, proposed by the Russian psychologist Lev Vygostsky.[45] For children to develop, Vygostsky argued, parents should provide them with challenges that test their abilities but scaffolded in such a way as to not be overwhelming. This zone represents the optimal balance. In that way the child can gradually develop greater competence. It's a lesson in life that we can all continue to learn from because when you push yourself within near boundaries, you progress, generating a sense of achievement and happiness at your accomplishment. If you never push yourself or if you reach too far beyond your ability, you will not grow.

Vygostsky also identified the way children internalise parental support and social exchanges provided by caregivers in the form of egocentric, private speech. He argued that during structured play and tuition, the child was creating an internal model of the adult advice and encouragement. If you watch young children alone at play, especially pretend play with their dolls, they often have a running commentary about what is going on.[46] It can be charming to eavesdrop on these private conversations. They may say, 'Well done, Sally' or 'Silly Billy' as they reflect on their own activities or pass judgement on their toys.

Children initially ramble on in their private speech when it first appears at around two to three years, but as they mature, the private speech becomes more task-focused as a way of directing their thought patterns. This interpretation is supported by the finding that children perform better at problem-solving tasks when they use private speech as a way of planning their actions. Over time, at around five to seven years of age, the child learns to internalise these instructions as self-directed inner speech.

This inner voice becomes the inner conversation that most of us continue to experience as adults and which makes up most of the conscious conversation we have with ourselves in our minds. Sometimes it helps to speak out this inner voice as a way of directing our plan of action. My elderly mother still does this when she is trying to solve some practical problem. When I recently watched her cooking in her kitchen, she gave a running commentary of the various actions: 'Okay, let's see what this is like. Yes, I think a little more salt is needed. Now, where did I put the salt?'

The inner voice can be a valuable tool when it comes to problem-solving, but also it can become the source of unhappiness when it ceases to help and, rather, hinders us. The psychologist Ethan Kross calls this aspect of the inner voice *chatter*, and it can take up a lot of mental effort and attention during the day.[47] Negative chatter refers to rumination, catastrophising and other self-defeating thoughts. Sometimes that inner voice can undermine our well-being by casting doubt or, worse, criticising us: 'You're not good enough. You're ugly.' It may prevent you from attempting a goal before you have even started it, because it warns you that you will fail. For some of us, our inner voice is really our own worst critic.

We all have this inner voice. It is an inescapable aspect of the human mind, so rather than trying to ignore it, it is better to harness its power, using it as a tool to control our thoughts. You can take that critical voice and turn it into a supporter, and one way to do that is through the practice of *distancing*.

Psychological distancing

Left to our own devices, when we focus on our problems, we tend to blow them out of proportion. Part of this is due to the negativity bias we described in the last lesson, and it's also due to our tendency to ruminate or listen to our inner critic. Because of our egocentric minds, we tend to immerse ourselves in the problem and amplify it. Like an emotional black hole, we are sucked into the centre of our problem. This is where putting a distance between our self and the problem is beneficial. Let me demonstrate with a positive psychological intervention that makes us think more allocentrically.

I want you to consider a problem that is currently bothering you. A real problem – not a hypothetical one or a fictitious fantasy. It may not be in your consciousness right now, but dig down and find me something in your psyche that makes you unhappy. I am sure you'll be able to find one. I want you to introspect again – to turn the spotlight of your attention inwards to examine the contents of your own mind. Find this problem of yours and reflect upon how it makes you feel in the present moment. For example, in the service of full disclosure as I type these words, mine would be something like:

> 'I am worried that no one will read my book because I'm not sure that it's good enough and that upsets me after all the time and effort I put into writing it.'

Now, your turn. If you are in a public place, then speak silently to yourself, using your inner voice. If you are alone, then you can say out loud:

> 'I am worried about [whatever it is] because [whatever the reason may be] and this makes me upset.'

Take a moment to examine your emotional reaction to what you have just said to yourself. How does that make you feel? I expect you don't feel too great because I have reminded you about a problem, made you focus on it, express your unhappiness about it and then try to get you to examine your feelings. And now that I have reminded you of your problem, it is now in the forefront of your thoughts. 'Thanks for nothing,' you say. Don't worry, because I have a quick fix.

Do exactly the same thing again, but this time don't use any first-person terms like 'I' or 'me'; rather, talk about your worry in the third person. Again, in my case, it would be:

> 'Bruce is worried no one will read his book because he's not sure that it's good enough and that upsets him after all the time and effort he put into it.'

Now, your turn. Use your name and talk about your problem in the third person.

How does that feel compared to before? If you do indeed have a real problem that worries you and you followed the instructions to the letter then, in all likelihood, you will feel better after talking about your problem in non-first-person terms. Nine out of ten people in the audiences I regularly try this exercise on, when reflecting upon their problems in the non-first-person, find the experience much less negative than talking about problems in the first person. This technique is based on a phenomenon known as *psychological distancing*.[48]

Reflecting upon an unresolved problem from a non-first-person perspective reduces its negative emotional impact. This happens because referring to yourself in the non-first-person automatically transports you out of the egocentric perspective and into one that is more allocentric, thereby putting a psychological distance between you and your problem.[49] Unless we are royalty, we rarely refer to ourselves in the third person, but we almost exclusively use names to refer to other people. So, when Bruce talks about Bruce, he is thinking about Bruce from a distance.

Psychological distancing when referring to yourself in the non-first person is a bit like comforting or consoling a friend with a problem. You may feel bad for a friend's problem but not as much as if it were your problem. Consistent with this altered perspective is the finding that psychological distancing influences the way the brain represents the concept of self. Using brain-imaging to measure blood flow, Ethan Kross instructed participants to use their inner voice to speak either in the first or non-first person when reflecting upon a personal negative memory of an event.[50] Those instructed to use their own name showed lower activation in the mPFC part of the DMN than those who used the first-person pronoun, 'I'. In other words, the representation of self in the brain regions usually associated with that concept was flattened by adopting non-first-person language.

Another way to use psychological distancing is to mentally time-travel to consider the situation from the perspective of both your past and future selves. If you are currently worrying about a problem, first try to remember where you were one or five years ago. In all likelihood, you will have moved on, or the problem you had in the past no longer exists. Think of the things that were not working in your life and how you have since overcome them. Reassure yourself that you will eventually overcome your immediate problem.

Then try mentally time-travelling to the future. Imagine how important that problem will be in one or five years from now. When you project yourself into the future, you introduce a psychological distance of time. We know from experience that 'time is a great healer' and this technique forces us to take the long-term perspective, which invariably is more positive.

The ability to project ourselves into the past or the future is essential to help us gain perspective. If we let ourselves succumb to mind-wandering and the associated dangers of rumination or critical inner voices, then we are likely to be unhappy. This is an overly egocentric self, wallowing in self-pity or negative evaluation. The more distance we can put between our self and our problems, the better we will be able to cope.

Another way to achieve perspective, and one that fits with the evolved need to connect with others, is to strengthen our relationships. In the next lesson, we will discover that our relationship with others impacts directly on our own thoughts and behaviours in ways that are often subtle and out of our control. We will consider how to get the best out of others in order to boost our own happiness. It requires the understanding of not only others' thoughts but also our own, and why we are so often at odds with what people are really thinking about us. We may be social animals but, increasingly, we seem challenged in the relationships we form. Part of this problem stems from our overly egocentric bias, but also from some gross inaccuracies and predictions about how much we will enjoy the company of others.

Happiness exercises

Be aware of rumination. Take note of when your mind is wandering and acknowledge when there is a tendency towards negative thoughts. If this happens, try distraction or engage in an activity that requires concentration.

Remember the consequences of ironic suppression. Try not to actively suppress negative thoughts but rather accept when they appear. Treat them as foreign objects and let them go. If thoughts are keeping you awake, get up and undertake some activity until the thoughts dissipate.

Try meditating on a regular basis. It may not be for everyone but give it a go. Five minutes a day is all you need. Start with a guided meditation, which is the easiest way to regain control over your mind.

Find your flow. Take on challenges or hobbies that match your abilities. Try those that push you that little bit extra, because this is the way to learn and improve.

Practise self-distance. Use non-first-person language to introduce a psychological distance between yourself and your problems. Write down any problems you have and then review the situation as if you were a friend giving yourself advice. If you are currently unhappy about something, then project yourself into the future, one year or five years from now. This should make the current situation seem more temporary and transient.

LESSON SIX

Connect with Others

So far, we have linked happiness to becoming more allocentric and less egocentric. This is partly due to the negative distortions and biases that the self creates – the disadvantages of what psychologist Mark Leary calls 'the curse of self'.[1] The self may enable all manner of useful strategies, such as simulating other people's minds or predicting our futures, but left to its own devices, the self can become bedevilled by negative thinking when drawing comparisons and imaging potential problems. Egocentrism is the default mode for our stream of consciousness and our experience of self. Even if we manage to suppress the tendency for rampant egocentric thinking, it remains latent or dormant, waiting to reappear when it is least welcome. Stress, pressure and anxiety trigger egocentric thinking in adults,[2] which, in turn, amplifies problems in a negative feedback loop. The more anxious we are, the more likely we are to withdraw from social interactions with others and become isolated.[3] Over time, we become more miserable and detached from the very things that will help us feel happier.

If you can't easily become less egocentric intentionally, then one simple way to shift your perspective is to connect with others. Deliberately direct the focus of your attention towards those around you. Turn your spotlight outwards, not inwards. As we noted in the meditation exercises in Lesson Five, if we can control our attention, this prevents intrusive thoughts that are caused by a limited attention span. If we direct our attention towards others, we become less self-focused by default. We may be able to switch between self and others quickly, but we can't simultaneously occupy both perspectives. Ask any new parent or pet-owner. When you have dependents that you care about, you automatically shift out of your egocentric bias. When they can't tell you what is wrong, you have to deploy your theory of mind to figure out what's going on in their head. Why are they crying? What are they thinking? What is it that they need? When you look after another living thing that requires care and attention, you necessarily become less egocentric.

In this lesson, we will examine our relationship with others and how we can benefit from increasing our social connectedness. We evolved as a hyper-social animal, but there are barriers to overcome in our attempts to form meaningful connections with others. As we will discover, we often think that the acts of making connections and starting conversations are more awkward than they really are, and we also wrongly assume that we will be rejected. These are misconceptions that we'll consider ways to improve upon.

Social connectedness is also becoming increasingly hard in our ever-changing world. It is well recognised that loneliness is on the rise in developed countries, with all the negative consequences this brings for happiness and physical health.[4] As we saw in Lesson Two, before the arrival of agriculture, humans evolved to live and thrive in relatively small nomadic groups for hundreds of thousands of years. That lifestyle has been changing since the beginning of civilisation, and with it, so have our interactions with each other. We are now at a pivotal point in human development as modernity and digital innovations are shaping the way we behave and the worlds we may occupy. We are increasingly living in more densely packed cities but, paradoxically, we are becoming more isolated. A 2015 YouGov poll showed that, in the UK, despite the proximity of living more closely together, less than a third of people living in urban areas know all five of their nearest neighbours' names, compared to over half of residents in rural areas.[5]

Then there are the variations in a sense of cohesion and community, which vary nationally.[6] We will also look more closely at those nations that seem to be getting it right when it comes to its citizens' happiness. For example, why are the Nordic countries the happiest places to live?

In this penultimate lesson, we examine connecting with others as a crucial route to becoming happier. We will explore what is going on in the brain when we are with others and why sociality impacts on our mental well-being. We will consider how our environments shape our friendliness and why we are so wrong in thinking about others when it comes to predicting how much they will like us. In this lesson we will consider the secret sauce of social connection when it comes to pursuing happiness.

Good vibrations

Shared experiences amplify our pleasure. Whether it is playing music, playing sport or simply playing around, when we do it together, it is so much more fun than when we do it alone. In one study where participants had to rate the flavour of chocolate, they found it tastier when there was another person present eating chocolate at the same time, as opposed to having another person present but doing some other activity like reading a magazine.[7]

Joint activities are even more enjoyable, and significantly more rewarding, when they are synchronised – where individuals coordinate their actions together like dancing. Even unpleasant experiences are more tolerable when undertaken in groups, which is why synchronised physical training has been found to elevate pain thresholds among rowers when they exercise together, compared with exercising alone.[8]

Most forms of positive social interaction require noting what others are doing and then timing our responses in an appropriate way. Whether you are making out or simply making conversation, you need to coordinate. Without synchrony, things don't seem quite right. One of the challenges of video-conferencing technology, as many of us discovered during the recent pandemic lockdown, is that timing-delays and glitches can create awkward conversations with frequent interruptions to the flow of communication.[9] The non-verbal communication we use to facilitate social interactions also relies heavily on coordinated and synchronised signals that we are acutely sensitive to. We may not even be consciously aware of the lack of synchrony, but we can recognise that something is missing.

The good vibrations were absent, and we say that the other person was giving off a 'bad vibe'.

Synchronisation is a foundation for social connectedness and has been present in human pastimes, in the form of chanting, singing, dancing or drumming, since time immemorial. When the timing is perfect, the whole is greater than the sum of its parts and becomes transcendent, which is why synchronised behaviours feature in most important ceremonies.[10] These synchronised actions are at the core of human ritual and found in every culture. Making music is one of the earliest cultural activities that involved others. The oldest musical instrument is a 60,000-year-old bone flute that was made not by modern humans, but by our cousins, the Neanderthals. Some of the earliest cave paintings, at the Bhimbetka rock shelters in Central India, from around 10,000 years ago, depict dancers. Even babies enjoy dancing with someone else in synchrony. Fourteen-month-olds, carried around in a baby sling, were found to prefer dancing with another who moved in tempo to the Beatles classic 'Twist and Shout', compared with someone who danced out of time to the music. After the session, each dance partner 'accidentally' dropped an object that was out of reach. The infants who had danced with the synchronised partner were much more likely to spontaneously come to their assistance, compared to those infants who had the lousy dance partner.[11]

Caregivers and babies often engage in musical activities together, such as singing, clapping, dancing and bouncing, which actively promotes prosocial behaviours. This early experience of synchrony stays with us as we develop. We are more cooperative as young children and adults after an episode of synchronised activity with another. We are even more generous. In a study of adults, one group of participants were instructed to move their bodies in synchrony to the same beat of a metronome that they listened to through headphones, while another group had the same brief but were played different beats of the metronome, which produced asynchronous movements.[12] In a subsequent game where each member could contribute money (up to $5) to a shared resource, those who worked together towards a synchronised goal were more generous to the group and felt closer to other members. On average, over half of those in the synchronised group contributed the full $5, whereas only a fifth did so in the asynchronous group.

We feel good when we synchronise with others, which is why social gatherings, dancing, music, ceremonies and performances are just some of the peculiar human behaviours that make us happy. What is remarkable is that synchronisation takes place between individuals not only in their body movements, but also in their brain activity when they are engaged in a mutual experience. For example, synchronised firing can be measured in the neural activity of the individual brains of audience members watching emotionally charged movies, indicating that emotions operate like a binding or coupling mechanism.[13] Like a guitar string that will start to vibrate when you strike a tuning fork, our brains can be in tune with one another.

The degree of synchronisation is also a measure of shared understanding. Princeton neuroscientist Uri Hasson scanned the brains of individuals using fMRI imaging while they were telling a story or listening to one told by another.[14] Once they had taken into consideration the time delay of the speaker uttering the sentence and the listener comprehending the speech, they found synchronised neural coupling, as if the two brains were working together to achieve mutual understanding. When the sentences were jumbled so that all meaning was removed, the synchronisation disappeared. Neural coupling was also absent when the speaker was talking in Russian to non-Russian-speaking listeners. When both the speaker and listener communicated in English, the extent of the neural coupling predicted how much of the story was understood by the listener – not just the words, but the overall meaning.

Why do we like synchronised social interactions? In the brain, joint activities like making music and dancing have been linked to the release of *endorphins*, the pleasure chemicals of the brain that form part of its own natural opioid system, which is enhanced when activities are undertaken together as a group.[15] For example, singing in a choir decreases levels of cortisol.[16] We feel closer, kinder and more connected to others during these activities, but we also feel different about ourselves. One consequence of synchrony is a blurring of the boundaries between self and others, which generates a sense of oneness with the group. This represents a shift from ego-centric self-focus to a more allocentric perspective, the main theme of this book. One meta-analysis of synchrony found the following pattern of effects that shows this shift produces four positive benefits:[17] first, synchrony encourages prosocial behaviours such as willingness to help others; second, it makes us feel connected to others; third, we become more aware of what they may be thinking; and fourth, it increases mental well-being. In short, when we do things together in synchrony, we act and think about the other person more, which increases our sense of connectedness and therefore makes us happier.

How can we improve our synchrony with others? We have already talked about group activities such as dancing or taking part in some experience as an audience, but these are occasional events. One activity that we all engage in on a regular basis is face-to-face conversations. Put your smartphone away for a start. Studies show that just the visibility of smartphones detracts from the enjoyment of social interaction.[18] When you are on your phone, not only are you not mutually engaged in a joint activity, but your attention is entirely elsewhere. Not everyone feels like this about smartphone etiquette, but prioritising your phone tells others that you consider them less important than your own interests.

You should also practise active listening. Try listening more than you talk, and you'll soon discover the conversation goes better when it goes in both directions. Listening increases trust and engagement, and those who actively 'listen to understand' have better and happier relationships with others.[19] In one brain-imaging study, subjects rated those who practised active listening as more likeable, and this was associated with neural activation in reward areas of the brain's *ventral striatum*.[20] That's not to say you should remain silent. Focus on what is said and ask relevant questions to show you are engaged. Be positive about the other person and try to establish a rapport with constructive feedback. As a result, you will be liked and rated more positively by the other person, making the experience happier for everyone involved. When you direct your attention towards others, this will improve the quality of the social interaction, and synchrony should arise naturally.

The empathic brain

One of the most popular episodes of the cult science fiction TV series *Star Trek*, called 'The Empath', was broadcast in the US in 1968 but banned from the BBC in the UK until the 1990s for its portrayal of torture. The empath in question was an alien who took on the pain and suffering of others to help them. We humans also empathise when we watch others being physically hurt, which is why graphic violence is routinely the source of audience complaints and why the BBC censors deemed the *Star Trek* episode unsuitable for viewing.

One reason why we can feel the suffering of others is that our brains resonate emotionally in the same way as they do when we are engaged in synchronised movements. There are circuits in our brains that mirror the emotions of others – especially those primary emotions of sadness, happiness and fear. As we noted in Lesson Four, negative emotions are reliably stronger than positive ones, and so most of the early research focused on the effects of witnessing the suffering of others during painful procedures. A summary of all the studies into how we respond to painful experiences has revealed that the same pain areas of the brain's *anterior insula* and the *anterior cingulate cortex* are consistently activated during the experience of our own pain and when feeling vicariously the suffering of others.[21]

Witnessing another's suffering does not automatically trigger empathy, however.[22] Two people could witness the same suffering of another but have different empathic responses. On one end of the spectrum are psychopaths, whose empathic brain regions do not light up when they imagine others in pain as they do in neurotypical people.[23] At the other end of the spectrum, there are so-called 'super empaths', who overly experience the emotions of others and feel too much. When they watch videos of others being injected with a needle or scratching, they report physical sensations in the same regions of their own bodies.[24] Watching a boxing match would be too overwhelming for them. The neural response of super empaths to observing another's suffering is much greater than the rest of the population's. One intriguing explanation for this difference is that where most of us can register another's emotional state, our response remains suppressed or inhibited, and so does not cross the threshold into our awareness.[25] In the super empath, this gating mechanism fails. Another related explanation is that super empaths have a blurred sense of the distinction between self and other, and so when they say, 'I can feel your pain', they may be telling the truth, because they have a weaker boundary between self and others.

When one loses the distinction between self and other, there is a danger of *empathic distress*.[26] This can adversely affect those who encounter distress on a regular basis as part of their job and explains why some seem to switch off when faced with others' suffering. In her thirty-year career as a vet, Trisha Dowling sometimes had to euthanise pets, which is often traumatic for the owners.[27] As a pet-owner herself, Trisha recognised the importance of distinguishing between her client's grief and her own personal grief when she had lost her own animals. If she failed to draw that distinction, then there was the danger of empathic distress, a strong aversive and self-oriented response to the suffering of others that generated a desire to rush through the euthanasia procedure as quickly as possible. This could give the impression of indifference or not caring, which is one of the most common complaints regarding human healthcare encounters and communication.[28] What patients and their relatives often do not appreciate is that healthcare workers cannot afford to get emotionally invested. As a medical doctor, my wife Kim witnessed how many colleagues were unable to cope with the empathic distress of dealing with patients and relatives. Eventually they either moved into lab-based clinical research or left the field entirely.

Our response on the empathic spectrum depends on our biology interacting with our environments. Men are generally less empathic than women[29] and the heritability of empathy is similar to other personality dimensions, such as intelligence and happiness – which we have already discussed in the Introduction is at around 50 per cent and means there is plenty of scope for learning and the environment to shape empathy.[30] Emotional reactions to others' suffering is present from the start as newborns will cry more when they hear the crying of other newborns.[31] However, this crying is not empathic. Remember, the infant is egocentric, so it is unlikely that they are thinking about the well-being of other infants in the delivery ward. In contrast, older children and adults recognise the distinction between self and other, and feel a true sense of empathy and concern at the plight of others.[32]

We usually think of empathy as a positive personality trait because it demonstrates that we are registering the suffering of others, but there are also dark aspects of this behaviour. First, whether we display empathy, and how much of it we display, depends on who the object of our empathy is and the extent to which we identify with them. The greater the similarity in terms of sex, race and age, the more the empathic response.[33] Empathy is stronger for in-group members and weaker for out-group individuals, and so prejudice is embedded into our empathic responses.[34] If we don't care as much about the suffering of others, then this can give us cause to ignore their predicament. Whether we trust the other person also influences our empathy. After playing a game of trust involving money, male observers generated a weaker empathic neural response to watching those receive pain who had cheated on the game.[35]

Although empathy can generate distress, there is another more adaptive and positive way we can respond to the predicaments of others and that is through compassion. A leading player in this field of research is German neuroscientist Tania Singer, who draws the distinction between empathy and compassion. Both are triggered by the plight of others but, unlike empathy, which is self-focused, compassion is other-focused. She describes the difference as follows: 'In contrast to empathy, compassion does not mean sharing the suffering of the other: rather, it is characterised by feelings of warmth, concern and care for the other, as well as a strong motivation to improve the other's well-being. Compassion *is feeling for and not feeling with* the other.'[36]

Singer's research has shown that compassion can be learned and developed, which results in a host of benefits both to the individual and others. In a carefully designed study known as the ReSource Project,[37] Singer and her colleagues systematically evaluated the impact of different mental training programmes that targeted either mindfulness, compassion or mentalising skills. This was achieved using different forms of meditation and practising social interactions in face-to-face pairs on a regular basis over nine months. That's quite a commitment, but less than 8 per cent of over 300 participants dropped out, indicating that participants were benefiting from the experience. Many papers continue to emerge from the ReSource Project that have looked at behaviour, neuroimaging, responses to stress and so on, but the bottom line is that the most beneficial type of intervention is compassion training.[38] Compassion training not only promotes prosocial behaviour, but improves individual happiness and resilience, which in turn fosters better coping with stressful situations.

There are two components to this compassion training. The first is a particular type of meditation called the 'loving-kindness meditation' (LKM) that has its origins in ancient India. Individuals are first asked to relax, close their eyes and contemplate a person for whom they already feel warm and tender feelings (e.g., their child or partner). They are then asked to extend these warm feelings first to themselves and then to an ever-widening circle of others in a series of mantra statements. For example, the LKM could begin with instructing participants to recite 'May I be happy, may I be well, may I be at peace' eight times, with controlled breathing in between. Next, they are instructed to take that positive experience and think of a friend, repeating the phrase: 'May you be happy, may you be well, may you be at peace.' They might then think of a work colleague, and so on. Finally, they are requested to think of someone they may have difficulty with and repeat the exercise. The goal is to extend the positive feelings that begin with the self in ever-increasing reach to more distant people.

The second component of the compassion training in the

ReSource Project was a ten-minute face-to-face discussion with another person, where participants talked about anything that had happened the previous day that was challenging or had given them reasons to be grateful, or both. They simply had to discuss emotionally salient events. Even though they had a new partner each week, participants felt increasing connectedness through these exercises over time. This indicates that participants were adopting a new way of approaching the challenge of getting to know others, exposing and talking about their own vulnerabilities, and generally becoming more sociable and, in turn, likeable. Increased social connectedness leads to a greater sense of trust, which, as we will discover later in this lesson, is a fundamental component of well-being.[39]

Open up your mind

The net effect of the compassion training was to reduce the distance between self and others, without merging into an indistinguishable entity that would lead to empathic distress. In other words, it encouraged people to become less egocentric and more allocentric by opening up. This notion of opening up is consistent with the theory for improving well-being proposed by psychologist Barbara Fredrickson, known as the 'broaden and build' theory.[40] Fredrickson proposes that, as well as seeking happiness for ourselves, we should also promote positive states in others around us – not as an end-state, but rather to lay the foundations for increasing psychological growth and physical well-being over time.

As we noted in Lessons Four and Five, we have biases that preoccupy our thoughts, and these lead to a narrowing focus on potential threats. This is an evolved adaptive strategy to hone in on problems, but as we now live in increasingly complex worlds with many imagined threats, narrowing our focus may be counterproductive. In contrast to negative emotions, positive emotions broaden our attention, thoughts and behaviour, providing more opportunities to build resourcefulness. In one study by Fredrickson and colleagues, participants were randomly assigned to watch video clips either of penguins playing around or clips of fields, streams and mountains in warm, sunny weather, both to induce positive emotions.[41] Other participants watched a video clip from the film *Witness* where a group of young men taunt members of the Amish community. This clip generated negative emotions of anger and fear. They then had to perform a comparison task to judge which of two visual arrays were more similar to the target (Fig. 6.1).

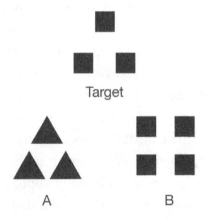

Fig. 6.1: Global-versus-local processing task. (Reproduced from Fredrickson and Branigan, 2005)

There is no correct answer. Pattern A has the same overall or group layout (pyramid) whereas pattern B has a different layout but the same individual (local) elements. Participants who viewed the positive-emotion videos tended to regard the triangular arrangement of pattern A as more similar to the target than pattern B. Those who answered B were being more focused. The interpretation was that the induction of positive mood made individuals more open, whereas the negative mood made them narrower and more focused.

In Fredrickson's model, positive moods lead to more expansive thinking, whereas negative moods lead to concentrating on details. This is an interesting perspective as we tend to think of happiness as carefree, whereas creative genius is born out of seriousness and tortured despair. However, the reverse appears to be true. If people are happier, they are more inventive and open to possibilities. For example, after positive-mood induction, participants can generate more novel associations for the word 'carpet', such as 'fresh' or 'flying', whereas those induced into a bad mood simply give the obvious associated word of 'rug'.[42] Negotiators in a good mood are more likely to reach a satisfactory settlement compared with those in a negative mood, because they are more flexible in their thinking and open to options.[43] The flexible thinking generated by positive moods means that people will be much more willing to consider different views, try new ideas and approach others. This in turn produces a positive feedback loop that makes individuals more liked and approachable, which is how the 'broaden and build' approach leads to increased well-being.

The Rice Hypothesis

Openness to others seems to vary depending on where you are in the world. I have lived and worked in many different places, and one thing that I and many have remarked upon is how friendly and open some peoples are compared with others. In the UK, the Scots, Irish, Welsh and Northerners are famously friendly in comparison to the Londoners in the South, who are much more reserved and less likely to speak to strangers. In the US, Southerners are known for their hospitality while Bostonians and New Yorkers are regarded as rude.

Of course, these are sweeping generalisations, but there do appear to be regional variations indicating that environment shapes how we behave towards one another. One representative sample of 400,000 UK residents found that high levels of agreeableness were prevalent throughout most of Scotland, as well as areas in the North, the South West of England and East Anglia, suggesting that disproportionate numbers of residents of these areas were friendly, trusting and kind.[44] However, the lowest levels of agreeableness were concentrated primarily in Central and Greater London, indicating that comparatively large proportions of residents of these areas were uncooperative, quarrelsome and irritable.

What is true of the UK is also true of other large countries with large populations, such as the US and China. Humans may all be one species, but we behave very differently across the world. Why are there these geographical differences? Do people who are more or less friendly move to these respective locations? Or is it the culture or environment that makes people friendly?

It is difficult to answer these questions, as culture, history, politics and a host of other factors contribute to the psychology of individuals living together, but there are some interesting accounts. As a student of behavioural science, Thomas Talhelm spent his graduate days in China, a vast country of over a billion people. Initially he lived in Guangzhou in the south and noted how, when he bumped into residents in the local busy supermarket, they would tense up, avoid eye contact, shuffle away awkwardly and avoid any conflict. They were shy around strangers and focused on avoiding conflict. However, when he visited Harbin in northern China, he noted how people behaved very differently. They were much more independent, confrontational and outgoing. Why were people from the two regions so different?

Talhelm came up with a broaden-and-build idea based on farming. Thinking about China, he noted that south of the Yangtze River, where the climate is warmer and rainfall more plentiful, farmers have been growing rice for at least 10,000 years, whereas north of the river they grow wheat.[45] The crops differ significantly in how they are farmed. Rice is twice as labour-intensive compared with wheat and requires irrigation.[46] An irrigation system quadruples the rice yield but it is beyond the capability of a single farmer to build or maintain one. A single family cannot provide enough labour to survive by farming rice and so success depends on the collective effort of farmers. Irrigation also has to be shared, as the same water supplies neighbouring farms. Therefore, rice farming requires cooperation and generates shared accountability and interdependence in comparison to wheat farming. Could these different farming practices influence the communities' behaviour?

When he looked at various psychological measures of different styles of thinking, Talhelm found there was a wheat–rice divide as predicted, with those from the wheat regions in the north scoring higher on scores of psychological individualism.[47] Individualism emphasises the individual and his or her rights, independence, and relationships with other individuals. For example, in a measure of implicit or unconscious individualism, participants from wheat- and rice-growing communities were asked to draw circles in a network that represented themselves and their friends in what's called a 'sociogram'. For example, in the sociogram network below (Fig. 6.2), I am friends with Mel, Laurie and Paul. Laurie and Paul are also friends but not with Mel. In this example, I have chosen to draw myself larger than the other members of the network.

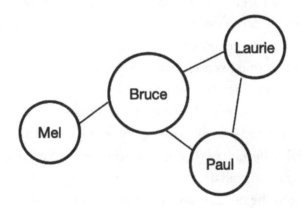

Fig. 6.2: An example of a sociogram that illustrates the connectedness of individuals within a social network.

When asked to draw the same type of sociogram, those from the wheat-growing regions drew themselves as larger than their friends, whereas those from the rice regions drew themselves as smaller than their friends. Typically, those from individualistic countries such as the US and the UK draw their self as larger, whereas those from collectivist societies, such as Japan where the tendency is to view oneself as a member of a larger (family or social) group, rather than as an isolated, independent being, draw their themselves as smaller.[48] Thinking in the individualistic wheat regions was also more analytical and focused, compared with the thinking of those from the collectivist rice-growing regions. This pattern was not restricted to China. The same agricultural–psychological divide was also found in India, another large country where rice and wheat are grown in different geographical regions.[49]

Other measures outside of the lab also fitted with the pattern of individualism in the wheat regions and collectivism in the rice areas. Divorce rates are typically higher in individualistic societies,[50] and indeed this was true for the wheat-growing regions of China. Even the way people conducted themselves in public when they thought they were relatively unobserved showed this difference between individualism and collectivism. Talhelm and his colleagues went into local Starbucks cafés in several different northern and southern Chinese cities to observe the naturalistic behaviour of customers in the café.[51] People from the northern, wheat regions were more likely to be sitting alone (35 per cent) compared with those in the southern Starbucks branches (20 per cent). Researchers in the various Starbucks branches then deliberately moved chairs to partially block the aisle, to see how customers reacted to the obstacle. Based on previous observations, the prediction was that people from individualistic cultures would be more likely to change elements of the environment to amend the situation, whereas those from more collectivist cultures would be more likely to change themselves to accommodate the situation. Only three out of 100 (3 per cent) customers from the rice region moved the chairs, preferring to squeeze through the gap, in comparison to 20 per cent of those from the wheat regions, who moved the chairs out of the way.

As individualism is one of the main defining characteristics of Western industrialised nations, its rise has been linked to economic growth. However, the rice hypothesis explains why individualism cannot simply be a consequence of individual wealth resulting from modernisation. Some of the wealthiest countries in the world are rice-growing countries in East Asia, such as Japan, Taiwan, South Korea and Singapore; they are less individualistic than they should be, given the patterns found throughout the rest of the world. The common factor among these nations is that they are all traditional rice cultures or colonised by those from rice cultures.[52]

The important thing to note is that individuals assessed in these studies were not themselves farmers but, rather, the descendants of families who had grown up within these communities. This is not biology at work but a result of parenting and culture. The differences observed were transmitted during child development, but parental influence is changing as the world opens up and there is more exposure to different views. A recent study of first-generation British Bangladeshi immigrants and second-generation British Bangladeshis raised in the UK reveals that while the traditional collectivism found in the immigrants is passed down vertically to their children, the children also acquire more individualistic ways of thinking, horizontally from their classmates and from the ubiquity of social media.[53]

Trust me

Our happiness depends on our relationships. And when it comes to human social relationships, trust is the most important ingredient. Trust is the willingness to take a risk or make oneself vulnerable with the expectation that the other party will reciprocate and not take advantage. When two people trust each other, they are freed from competition and strengthened by mutual interest. Without trust, relationships are doomed. Without trust, you can't be certain that others won't exploit you, and this places you in a constant state of vigilance and concern. Violation of trust between romantic partners, or cheating, is considered the most painful form of betrayal and its vengenace is the leading cause of spousal murders. What is remarkable is that when a murder is deemed a 'crime of passion', most courts of law in the UK and the USA will give the perpetrator a reduced sentence, such is the importance we place on trust in a relationship.[54]

In functional families, young children, who are wholly dependent on others, implicitly trust their parents. An important part of our social development is learning who else to trust, and the degree of trust depends on the closeness of the relationship. The further away the parties are in a relationship, the less trust there is and the more we depend on regulations and laws to ensure that everyone abides by the rules. Banking, healthcare, education and commerce are all built on the promise of trust but enforced by legislation.

We place our trust in others because we are a social species that needs to cooperate to survive, and that cooperation often involves vulnerability. To combat this, humans have evolved ways of establishing trust. If you think back to the origins of social connections in our evolution that we discussed in Lesson Two, you'll remember that it is the mechanism of reciprocal altruism that forged the bonds of mutual trust. We even have special sensitivity to detect those who cheat without having to think too hard.[55] For example, we are quicker to identify those who violate rather than conform to social rules.

Trust is so important that we would willingly pay to punish those who transgress it, even though we may be disadvantaged by the cost of doing so. For example, in a study involving economic games where adults were given the opportunity to contribute to a pot of money to benefit the group when it was shared out, there was the danger that some individuals might not contribute equally but still benefit at the pay-out.[56] Initially the game was played anonymously, but then, after each round, any cheaters were identified and the other group members were given the opportunity to 'fine' them by paying for the opportunity for retribution. Even though it came at a personal cost, members were willing to pay for the privilege of punishing the cheats. Over successive rounds, however, the cheating disappeared, indicating that such *altruistic punishment* operated to remove cheating as a strategy. These sorts of economic games in the lab reveal that trust is essential for group cohesion.

Trust among individuals and groups in the real world varies, which has implications for the quality of societies. Harvard economist Robert Putnam was interested why, in Italy, there was such variation between regions in terms of corruption and efficiency when it came to local services. He concluded that successful societies depended on networks, relationships, norms, values and informal sanctions – a set of factors that he captured in the term *social capital*.[57] When these are in place, residents are more likely to live in harmony and obey the rules. Communities with high social capital have lower crime rates, better education and do well economically. The ingredients of social capital are engagement, accountability and – most importantly – trust.

Many societies today are multicultural, which means that there are different groups who have the potential to come into conflict. We identify with our 'in-group' as being distinct from others, who belong to the 'out-group'. However, social capital emerges as the balance in trust that arises through in-group bonding and out-group bridging. Both are necessary and serve different purposes. Bonding is the trust that arises from interpersonal relationships that exists between closely knit groups, such as friends and families. These are the people most likely to help you out of a personal crisis or come to your aid. It can be regarded as the glue that binds individuals together. Out-group trust is more like a lubricant or cushion, reducing tension between different groups and communities that tend to be divided.[58] In modern society, genuine out-group trust is more important than in-group trust because institutions and organisations that maintain the cohesion and integrity of complex society work best when different groups cooperate and contribute equally. When these state institutions are operating efficiently, out-group trust can diminish the dependency of individuals on their friends and family by empowering them.

Empowerment and trust are key to the smooth functioning of society and therefore key to happiness. Empowerment opens up people's cooperation with out-groups which increases trust, stimulating societal cohesion and economic growth, which, over time, increases happiness. For example, the 2020 World Happiness Report identified that the five Nordic countries of Finland, Denmark, Norway, Sweden and Iceland have topped the happiness league tables for the past ten years. Not only are the citizens happier, but these countries are also less corrupt, safer, more cohesive and more equal on a number of measures of human development. They also have higher personal taxation to pay for social care support in terms of healthcare, employment and family benefits but it seems to be a price worth paying if it creates greater social cohesion.[59]

It is true that money is important to well-being, but it is not the wealthiest nations that are the happiest. Rather, it is those countries where the citizens are most trusting. In 2019, in a bizarre test of civic honesty, 17,000 wallets containing money were dropped in public places in 355 cities across forty countries to determine what percentage would be handed in.[60] Top of the honesty league tables were Switzerland, Norway, Netherlands, Denmark and Sweden, with 70–80 per cent of people handing in the wallet. As noted above, these are also the same countries that regularly top the list of the happiest countries in the world. Lower down on the trust table were wealthier countries like the US and the UK, with China at the bottom. Again, by comparison, these countries are also lower down on the happiness tables. These of course are only correlations, but they do suggest a relationship that seems intuitive – that trust is foundational to higher levels of happiness. Moreover, as part of the World Values Survey that has been conducted over the past thirty years, respondents are asked the following question: 'Generally speaking, would you say that most people can be trusted, or that you can't be too careful in dealing with people?' Authors of the various reports consistently find that 'individuals with high social and institutional trust levels are happier than those living in less trusting and trustworthy environments'. They also report that those who are happier live longer, are more cooperative, generally better able to meet life's demands and, again, are more trusting.[61]

Making friends

We all need trusting relationships for our happiness, if only to avoid the perils of loneliness. However, building relationships is a skill that many of us seem to lose with age. In 2018, the 'Be More Us' campaign to end loneliness produced a powerful video of young children making friends with solitary adults seated in a café.[62] The video begins with the question, 'Have we forgotten how to make friends?' and then shows how awkward adults are when they are approached by young children who want to befriend them. The children ask questions like, 'Why are you sitting alone? Where are your friends?' Very soon, the innocent questions disarm the elderly adults, who open up and become friendly. This, of course, is contrived, but it does make the point that as adults, we tend not to interact with strangers, whereas children are very happy to strike up conversations with anyone.

Modern life is full of opportunities to strike up a conversation. Urban dwellers live and work together in close proximity, but it is remarkable that some of the most densely populated urban areas are also some of the least friendly.[63] Urban modernisation does increase wealth (and wealth is associated with increased happiness) but, paradoxically, levels of happiness in larger urban cities are lower than in smaller communities. One reason is that strangers in close proximity routinely ignore each other.

In 2016, American Jonathan Dunne embarked on a campaign to persuade London Underground commuters to talk to each other by handing out badges emblazoned with the invitation 'Tube Chat?', with the intention that this would initiate conversations.[64] Reaction to this campaign was very negative, with *The Guardian* newspaper claiming that Tube Chat had 'provoked horror among commuters' and led to the setting-up of a rival 'Shut Up!' campaign[65] with an account on social media. The opposing campaign's founder, Londoner Brian Wilson, even handed out a rival badge with the slogan 'Don't Even Think About Talking to Me!' and the instructions 'Let them know you'd rather drink a pint of bleach than talk with them!' The Tube Chat campaign ended up being a flop as only one in five commuters accepted one of Dunne's badges. Are Londoners really so unfriendly? The following year, a YouGov poll showed that two thirds of Londoners would prefer not to talk to fellow commuters, but this is also true for around half the population in other large cities.[66]

Some of us actively avoid social interaction. Another American, the introverted journalist Jessica Pan, wrote an account of a year she spent forcing herself to socialise, called *Sorry I'm Late, I Didn't Want to Come.*[67] Like many who shun social interactions, she used her introvert label to excuse herself from going out but soon realised that her life of self-care and nights in was in fact self-limiting, as she recognised the opportunities she was missing out on. Pan threw herself into the deep end of social connection, from using friendship apps to giving a stand-up comedy routine at the Edinburgh Fringe festival. As an introvert, she predicted that she would hate these experiences, but ultimately Pan came to appreciate the real benefits of connecting with others. When it comes to social interaction, sometimes we need to challenge our assumptions. By avoiding opportunities to connect, we may be compounding our own unhappiness by isolation.

In an influential 2014 study entitled 'Mistakenly seeking solitude', psychologists Nicholas Epley and Juliana Schroeder reported on a series of studies investigating attitudes to striking up a conversation among Chicago commuters, and the effect that these spontaneous interactions have on well-being.[68] As we've seen in Jonathan Dunne's campaign, people in large cities rarely talk to each other while commuting; they actively try to distance themselves from fellow travellers. Epley and Schroeder wanted to know why we behave like this. Is it because interacting with strangers is unpleasant and so we avoid it? Or is it because we mistakenly think that interacting with strangers will be unpleasant? When asked whether they would talk to a stranger in a waiting room, almost all of 203 respondents (93 per cent) said they would not. A large proportion (76 per cent) also said they would avoid talking to a stranger on a train.

In the Epley and Schroeder studies, research assistants approached commuters and asked them either to start a conversation with a stranger, sit in solitude or do what they normally do on their commute. They were handed a survey to complete at the end of their train ride. They also asked three additional groups of commuters to predict respectively what those different experiences would be like if they had to follow the same instructions. Results showed that on a scale of zero ('Not at all happy') to six ('Very happy'), commuters who were instructed to strike up a conversation with a stranger reported feeling much happier after their commute compared with the two groups, with the solitude group reporting feeling negative. This pattern of real responses was the complete opposite of the groups' who were simply asked to predict how they would feel if they had to speak to a stranger or were given the opportunity to be alone. In other words, we think that being left alone in solitude on our journey will be the most pleasant outcome and that having to talk to a stranger will be the worst, when in fact the reverse is true. One explanation verified in a later study was that commuters predicted that trying to engage in a conversation would be a negative experience, but when asked to imagine how they would feel after successfully completing the conversation, they were more positive.[69] In other words people know that it is good to talk, but the prospect of a failed attempt at a conversation is what prevents them making the effort in the first place.

One reason why people do not strike up a conversation is that they think that it will be considered rude and intrusive. They also worry that they may have nothing in common with the other person or, worse, that they will be ignored or rejected. This is not usually based on previous bad experiences. If everyone thinks like this, then this leads to *pluralistic ignorance* whereby everyone believes that others are less interested in striking up a conversation.[70] The same is true of trust and honesty. In the lost wallet study mentioned earlier, most people, including experts and non-experts, predicted much lower levels of honesty in returning the wallets. We tend to hold a poor view of our fellow citizens.

Pluralistic ignorance explains a liking gap that many of us have.[71] We think that people are not going to like us as much as they actually do. Even after the conversation, we underestimate how liked we were. Irrespective of whether it is strangers striking up a conversation, first-year university students getting to know each other, or members attending a workshop, people consistently think that they were not liked as much as they actually were by the other people.

People also overestimate how noticeable any of their supposed failings are. The so-called *spotlight effect* is the tendency to assume that other people notice our shortcomings more than they actually do.[72] In the original study of this phenomenon, college students were asked to wear bright-yellow Barry Manilow T-shirts to whichever class they were attending – something that was definitely not cool in this demographic. When asked to estimate how many other students noticed them wearing the conspicuous T-shirt, they thought that around half the class had noticed them when in fact it was only a quarter. We tend to overestimate how much others are paying attention to us and that distorts our objective comparisons. We all suffer from embarrassing moments, but the thing to remember is that most people do not even notice them. This is especially true when giving a presentation or performing in front of others. Although you may think that it is obvious, the audience does not know when you have screwed up.

It is ironic that we humans are social animals who depend

on each other for our physical and mental well-being and yet our number-one fear is other people. The fear of missing out, exclusion, ostracism, lack of respect, low self-esteem, public speaking, embarrassment and ridicule are just some of the socially relevant fears that terrify most of us. And yet, in most cases, these are illusory. They are mere projections that arise from our egocentric self. It may not be an easy thing to talk to strangers or form new friendships, but if you never try, you'll never discover just how much other people really like you.

Happiness exercises

Take part in more activities that provide opportunities for synchronicity. Rather than watching an event on television by yourself, invite friends around to watch it together. If you have the opportunity, take part in live events rather than televised ones. These experiences create memories to share with others.

Put away your smartphone during social interactions. Hide it in a pocket or in a bag. Phones are a distraction and undermine happiness. They also signal that your attention is not solely focused on the other person during a conversation.

Practise active listening. Pay attention to what the other person is saying. Talk less and listen more. Ask interesting questions and provide constructive criticism.

Learn to trust others. Start by sharing your own vulnerability. You could begin by saying, 'I am nervous to admit ...'

Strike up conversations with strangers. A good place to start is with those in hospitality such as waiting staff, where it is appropriate to have a conversation. Small talk is best to start with. You could try a compliment if appropriate. If they are unwilling to engage, do not persevere. Above all, exercise caution and safety – it's best to talk to someone new in a public space where there are others around.

LESSON SEVEN

Get Out of Your Own Head

In this book we have come to understand how humans evolved to be social beings, dependent on others for physical survival but also for our emotional sustenance. We start as helpless infants, in need of parents, to whom we are biologically wired to form emotional bonds. Initially these bonds are with our immediate family but then they extend to friends and others as we establish stable social identity and form groups over childhood. As individuals, we begin with a sense of self that starts off as egocentric but increasingly integrates with others, though our self-centred bias never entirely disappears. When we are threatened, stressed or under pressure, we revert to our egocentric self by becoming more self-focused. This is problematic because we worry and ruminate on negative thoughts whenever we focus on problems from our self-centred perspective. We seek to be happier, but we are thwarted by a brain that makes inaccurate judgements and pays special attention to negative information – especially anything that might threaten our social standing or lead to exclusion or isolation. Throughout this book, I have argued if we work on becoming less egocentric, we can reduce this negativity, strengthen our connections with others and improve our well-being. In this final lesson, I want to return to the message from Lesson One – that we should try to alter our ego as we consider some other approaches that could help us to become more allocentric. We do this when we connect with others, but we can also do it alone if we can get out of our own heads.

Tripping

The day Timothy Leary died in 1996, I was working in my office in the Department of Psychology at Harvard when there was a knock at the door. Leary, described by Richard Nixon as 'the most dangerous man in America', was notorious as the champion of psychedelic drugs in the 1960s.[1] As Leary had been a former psychology professor in my department before he was fired, an intrepid reporter from the *Boston Globe* had turned up asking for an opinion or quote from his former colleagues. Leary taught at the university long before my time, I explained, so I had neither a quote nor an opinion, but after the reporter had left, I reflected upon my own experience with psychedelics growing up as a teenager in Scotland twenty years earlier.

When I was fifteen, I took up metal-detecting as a hobby. I would spend hours in the local park digging up coins that had been dropped decades – and sometimes centuries – earlier. It is an absorbing pastime as it requires constant attention, listening out for any sudden change in tone to indicate a hidden treasure. Most of the time I was focused on the ground as I swept the head of the detector backwards and forwards, largely oblivious to anyone else – except for one day, when I noticed a bunch of older boys scanning the ground as if they were looking for something. Unless they are on an outing together, detectorists can be territorial creatures, and so I wandered up to challenge them, only to discover that they weren't searching for lost coins at all. What were they looking for? It turned out they were hunting for tiny hallucinogenic fungi known as 'magic mushrooms'.

At that time of my life, like most teenagers, I was experimenting. On discovering this natural, free – and at the time, legal – source of *psilocybin,* the mind-altering active ingredient, my own friends and I spent many evenings taking mushroom trips. Eventually I grew out of this behaviour, but I think my early experimenting with hallucinogenic mushrooms changed me.

If you have taken hallucinogens, then there is no need to explain what a psychedelic trip is like. If you have never taken hallucinogens, then there is still no way to explain what a psychedelic trip is like. But I'll give it a go. After the initial hour of gut-wrenching queasiness as the toxins take effect, there are rushes of warmth rising in your body like waves that reach an overwhelming feeling of euphoria. Different forms of intoxication can produce these sensations. But that's not what makes psychedelic tripping so life-changing.

During a trip, every component of your mind is altered – your sensations, perceptions, emotions and cognitions. Every conscious experience is distorted and intensified, and there are new opportunities for discovery. Things taste different, music

is more melodic, people are more beautiful, and nature is won-
drous. Everything seems magical and supernatural. Plants and
trees seem to breathe, as the natural world comes alive. There
is an overwhelming sense of joy. It's not just the euphoria but
a new way of experiencing reality that makes hallucinogens so
powerful. You marvel at the universe and everything in it. You
feel awakened, as if you have been living a mundane dream
and only now can you see everything clearly. You are connected to the cosmos. Psychedelic hallucination destroys your
normal, mundane sense of self that we have come to depend
upon in our daily lives.

Fast forward forty-five years, and I am a respectable psychology professor who no longer takes psychedelic drugs
and would not advocate that everyone should (as Leary did).
Psychedelics are certainly not for everyone. Apart from being
illegal (magic mushrooms were outlawed in the UK in 2005),
there are potentially harmful side effects upon the mental
well-being of some individuals, especially those who are prone
to generalised anxiety.[2] The hallucinations and distorted
sense of self produced by psychedelic drugs can generate depersonalisation and dissociative states. If, on the other hand,
you score high on personality traits of absorption, openness
and acceptance as well as a state of surrender – a willingness to
release one's goals, constructs, habits and preferences – then
you are more likely to have positive experiences or a 'good
trip'. A systematic review of the small but growing research
into the effects of psychedelic drugs revealed that these
were the traits that best predicted a 'mystical' experience.[3]
It is notable that these positive predictors are more akin to
a weaker ego and more allocentric perspective. Those who

approach psychedelics with a positive, open mindset in a state of surrender are also more likely to experience positive ego dissolution.

On the other hand, states and traits associated with preoccupation, apprehension and confusion, and an unwillingness to let go of a strong ego perspective, are more likely to lead to adverse reactions.

In spite of the potential downsides and adverse effects, there is increasing interest in psychedelics in clinical practice to treat depression and post-traumatic stress disorders that do not respond to conventional approaches. Under the correct supervision, where patient personality is first evaluated and there is informed consent, psychedelic-assisted therapy has been shown to be very effective. One clinical study reported that nearly three quarters (71 per cent) of patients with severe intractable depression showed significant improvement that lasted at least four weeks.[4] Unlike other medications and recreational drugs, psychedelics are a low risk for dependency and addiction, which makes them an appealing option for treatment. Starting in 2023, Oregon is the first US state to legalise psilocybin to enable patients to undertake psychedelic-assisted therapy, with other states, including Colorado, Connecticut and California, actively considering similar changes in their laws.[5] It seems that a psychedelic renaissance has arrived. However, although there are active psychedelic research programmes in other parts of the world, including London, UK, there are no immediate plans outside of those US states to make psychedelic drugs legal for clinical use, though their efficacy in treatments is being evaluated. The use of psychedelic-assisted therapy has become so polarised, with advocates and opponents on either side, that it is unlikely there will be a change in the UK law for the foreseeable future.[6]

One of the reasons psychedelics work clinically in the treatment of depression is that they impact on the brain mechanisms that generate our sense of self and others. Psychedelic drugs are often accompanied with mystical experiences, ego-dissolution and even ego-annihilation, including an increasing sense of connectedness with the cosmos. Brain-imaging studies have shown that *lysergic acid dithylamide-23*, more commonly known as LSD – a powerful synthetic hallucinogen similar to psilocybin – acts upon the default mode network we learned about in Lesson Five, which is consistent with the reports from those who have taken LSD – that it changes their sense of self and connection with others.[7]

The vivid experiences of an altered reality persist long after the effects of psilocybin have worn off. After psychedelic treatment, patients typically report tripping as a pivotal experience that has changed their outlook on life. I can still look at trees today and remember how they seemed to breathe and pulse with life under the influence of magic mushrooms. Those early experiences of losing my sense of self while on psychedelics had a profound impact that has stayed with me, both in my private and professional life. The temporary deconstructions that came with the trips made me aware that my sense of self was constructed.[8] For some that might be terrifying, but for me it was liberating and changed my whole outlook.

Find awe

Hallucinogenic drugs in various forms and preparations have been used throughout human history to achieve euphoric, altered states of mind, often during rituals and ceremonies.[9] But for those who are more cautious about taking psychedelic drugs or possess the negative traits that predict adverse reactions, or are simply law-abiding, less extreme states of altered self-representation can be achieved by other means. Around the world people engage in rituals like religious ceremonies that are geared to altering the sense of self without the use of drugs. The Whirling Dervishes are a Turkish Muslim order who perform a highly ritualised dance to achieve trance states by spinning anticlockwise with their right hand pointing upwards and their left hand pointing downwards as they chant the name of God. Each dancer wears a tombstone headpiece representing the ego and a white skirt symbolising the ego's shroud. The spinning symbolises the death of the ego and the union of the soul with God.

Other religious and secular ceremonies that include synchronised movements or group singing have also been shown to alter the sense of self and produce feelings of ecstasy. One of the best group activities for achieving these states, which also leads to cohesion and greater happiness, is joining a singing group or choir.[10] In a study, adults ranging in age from eighteen to eighty-three years were assessed for pain thresholds, happiness and feelings of connectedness to others before joining different classes on singing, creative writing or crafting.[11] Connectedness to others was measured on a seven-point 'Inclusion of Other in the Self Scale' (Fig. 7.2) that was a visual representation of the self–other relationship.[12] This representation of self and other as overlapping circles is another measure of relative egocentricism and allocentricism.

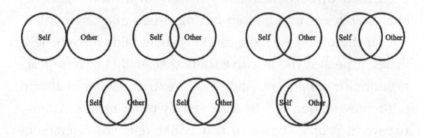

Fig. 7.2: The degree of overlap of self and other is a measure of relative egocentricism and allocentricism from the 'Inclusion of Other in the Self Scale'. (Adapted from Aron et al., 1992)

Groups were sampled shortly after the series of classes began and then again at three months and seven months later. All members in each of the different classes increased in their positive measures over the period, demonstrating the overall benefits of group activity, but the singers showed greater and more rapid increases in happiness and closeness to their classmates. Their egocentric self had shifted to merge more with others.

Self-altering activities are the basis of positive psychology interventions. If you consider the eighty-plus recommended activities from the Greater Good Science Center at the University of California, Berkeley[13] – the longest-established research-based group promoting positive psychology, going for over twenty years – then you will discover that most operate either directly or indirectly on our sense of self. Whether it is altruistic acts of kindness, or showing compassion or expressing gratitude, or more contemplative, solitary activities such as going for a walk in nature or sitting quietly in a meditative state, they all shift our perspective away from our ego and towards others. Even self-love, as it is known, where one treats oneself with more compassion, requires stepping out of the egocentric whirlpool of spiralling despair and looking at oneself more objectively, as you would with a friend. A bit like the psychological distancing we encountered in Lesson Five.

Another way to alter the self is to be impressed – by an external experience that impacts us emotionally. Impressive experiences can be so overwhelming or enthralling that they induce similar states of self-alteration. Standing in the Grand Canyon or looking through a telescope at the billions of stars in our Milky Way galaxy can make you feel small and insignificant.[14] One of the most profound experiences, known as the *overview effect*, occurs to the lucky individuals who have the opportunity to view our planet from outer space. Astronaut Edgar Mitchell described it as an 'explosion of awareness' and an 'overwhelming sense of oneness and connectedness ... accompanied by an ecstasy ... an epiphany'.[15]

We call such experiences 'awesome', though that term has rather lost its impact in everyday language, as just about anything can be described as awesome in vernacular conversation. Nevertheless, truly awesome experiences fill you with an overwhelming sense of wonder and amazement that lifts the spirit. You can get this from a piece of literature, drama or music, or by visiting Niagara Falls. In those moments of awe, we are not focused on ourselves. This is pleasurable not only because we are not thinking about our personal problems, but also because awe creates a greater sense of connectedness to something larger than our self.

In states of awe, we see things, including our personal problems, in perspective. In fact, there is evidence that people feel physically smaller during awesome experiences.[16] In a study of pensioners taking fifteen-minute weekly 'awe walks' in nature for over two months, not only did they report greater joy and prosocial positive emotions during their walks, but the photographs they took of themselves, or 'selfies', revealed that they took up less of the picture compared to a matched group who did not take awe walks and produced selfies which included more of their face.[17] As the pensioners took more walks in nature, their selfies became smaller and they reported increased feelings of being part of something larger than themselves. However, seeking out these experiences is not a sustainable strategy for growing happier because, as we discovered in Lesson Three, the brain is designed to get used to things. If you read the same book, watch the same movie, listen to the same piece of music, visit the same natural beauty spot or look at the night sky repeatedly, the awe will eventually wear off. One way to combat this familiarity is to make an effort to seek out new awesome experiences.

Another way to restore your capacity for wonder is to become more inquisitive, as children are. A study of children aged under five found that they ask an average of seventy-six to ninety-five questions per hour when talking to adults.[18] Asking questions stimulates a rapidly developing brain by trying to make sense of the world. The first questions usually begin with 'Why'. 'Why is it like that?' is a common question, but as the late, great Richard Feynman pointed out, there is no satisfying answer to 'why' questions. In one of the most insightful interviews, with over 1.5 million views on YouTube, an interviewer asked the Nobel-winning physicist how magnets worked,[19] and Feynman answered, 'They repel each other.' The exasperated interviewer asked, 'What does that mean, or why are they doing that, or how are they doing that? I think that is a perfectly reasonable question!' Feynman paused, took a deep breath, and replied, 'Of course, it's an excellent question. But the problem, you see, is when you ask why something happens, how does a person answer why something happens?' Feynman then went on to give a hypothetical example of asking why Aunt Minnie is in hospital. 'Because she broke her leg. Why did she break her leg? Because she slipped on ice. Why did she slip on ice? Because standing on ice is unstable. Why is standing on ice unstable?' and so on and so on. Feynman goes on to say, 'And you begin to get a very interesting understanding of the world and all its complications. If you try to follow anything up, you go deeper and deeper in various directions.' The point that Feynman makes is that there is a never-ending chain of explanations for any state of the universe. This kind of recursive questioning reveals the connectivity of the cosmos, which we never really think about because we spend much of the time focusing on ourselves in the here and now. If we take a moment and stop to think more deeply, we can feel more connected.

If you see an outstanding tree or old building, you can ask: how did it get there? Who planted it or built it? What was here before it? We have already discussed how mindfulness enables us to savour the moment more, but it can also be applied to asking deeper questions about our surroundings, even if we are non-scientists and non-historians. There is a joy to knowledge and understanding that seems to have been lost in the process of formal education and leading all too busy adult lives. Be a child again and discover wonder in the world.

Contemplative solitude

We need to think less egocentrically and be more other-oriented to become happier through our social connection. But we can also reduce our egocentrism when we are alone by immersing ourselves in contemplative thought or activities that produce serenity and calmness. Fertile solitude can be found when we are not burdened with intrusive thoughts arising from the problems around us. As the columnist Maria Popova has noted, scientists such as the father of neuroscience, Ramón y Cajal, and artists such as Bob Dylan, have extolled the virtues of solitude as opportunities for creative thought.[20] These moments are an oasis in our frenetic lives.

In Lesson Five we talked about achieving flow, the positive mental state that comes from absorption. Another approach is to seek out solitude at times when the modern world imposes upon us in a 24/7 demand for our attention. This is especially true when it comes to our digital devices, which are becoming an integral part of life that require constant response. Much of the digital economy revolves around us providing information that is harvested to develop and refine new markets. This requires our engagement, captured by clever systems designed to keep us online. Then there is the complexity of increasingly automated and inhuman systems that rule our lives. Texts, emails, passwords, resetting passwords, security checks and the cacophony of the fast-changing digital world can be overwhelming. I used to think that I was relatively technically savvy as I had learned how to program computers as a student, but as technology advances, I feel left behind.

Throughout this book, I have been advocating that we become less egocentric, but I don't think we can or should eradicate our self entirely. A recent review of the field of altered states of mind – induced either by drugs, mystical experiences or religious ceremony – concluded that well-being outcomes are better predicted by a sense of unity and connection than self-loss.[21] As already noted, self-annihilation can create a distressing sense of depersonalisation. The French psychologist Michael Dambrun has proposed that there does not have to be an either/or choice when it comes to the self.[22] It doesn't have to be 'me versus others' when it comes to happiness. Selfishness and selflessness are two sides of the same coin. Sometimes we treat ourselves and sometimes we treat others. Both activities can make us happy, but what is interesting is that the happiness we experience differs when we are in different modes of self-related behaviours.[23] Self-centred behaviour generates fluctuating happiness, whereas selfless behaviour directed towards others promotes more enduring, authentic happiness.

The reason that selfishness generates fluctuating happiness is that self-centred behaviours require establishing a well-defined sense of the self as distinct and separate to others. We consider ourselves as independent, better than others and worthy of the personal rewards that we give to ourselves. We know our own minds and we know what we want. We are motivated to obtain pleasure ('I'd really like an ice cream right now') and to avoid displeasure ('Better avoid that confrontation!'). These biases and favours may initially strengthen our ego, but these benefits are transient because as noted in Lesson Three, we readily and quickly adapt to such hedonistic pleasures. Thus, insight into our own happiness from the self-centred perspective provides ample opportunity to notice when it suddenly changes. Selfish goal-directed pursuits also depend on external circumstances that may be out of our control and can change rapidly ('Is the ice cream parlour open? Can I get someone to Uber the ice cream to me?'). Dependency on external circumstances means more opportunity for frustration, anger and hostility when goals are thwarted which is why self-centred rewards are more time-limited and context-dependent.

In contrast, selflessness is based on a weak distinction between self and others, and a greater sense of connectedness. Selflessness promotes the feeling of being in harmony with the environment (including others) and with oneself. Thus, happiness for the group is achieved by adapting and accommodating to others and environments in a less confrontational manner than if one was viewing the situation from only the ego perspective. As selflessness is less vulnerable to the vicissitudes of external circumstances, it produces more stable happiness. For these reasons, self-centred happiness will fluctuate much more at the individual level than at a group level. In other words, if we engage in pleasurable activities as individuals, the resultant happiness will wax and wane more quickly than the happiness derived from activities done in collaboration with others. For example, you might enjoy singing solo in the shower, but singing is all the more powerful when done as a member of a choir because you appreciate all the joy that others are experiencing as well as a sense of connectedness. This is supported by studies looking at levels of happiness using the 'experience sampling' technique, where individuals were contacted at random times in the week.[24] Not only were happiness levels derived from self-centred activities lower than those derived from group activities, but they were also found to fluctuate the most.

The final reason we experience more temporary, inauthentic happiness when acting selfishly is that we cannot fool ourselves. If we are both the purveyor and recipient of some positive experience, then we know when it ceases to make us happy. On the other hand, when we act for the group, we are not privy to the minds of others, and so we can continue to imagine that some, if not all, members still enjoy the positive benefits of the experience enacted for the group as a whole. By distributing the happiness among others, we are creating a more sustained and enduring hedonic shared experience. In short, you have the option to make yourself happy but it won't last as long as when you make other people happy, which in turn, will enrich the lives of both yourself and others for much longer.

Now that you have read my seven lessons for living well, you should now know that you can be happy by making others happy too. The trick is to find the right balance.

Happiness exercises

Rekindle your childhood curiosity. Ask more 'why' questions and rediscover the joy of learning. Seek out a deeper understanding of the everyday.

Take a walk around your neighbourhood. Look for interesting buildings or monuments. Think about them, and who built them and who lived in them. Try to find something that you have never noticed before. Take a trip to a National Park or any other awe-inspiring landscape. Mindfully pay attention to the experience. Some trees are hundreds of years old.

Go out and look up at the sky on a clear night to see the stars. Think about the vastness of space and time. Light from some of the stars you can see takes billions of years to reach Earth. The time it takes is older than our planet.

Each week, dedicate time to a hobby that brings you joy. Find others who enjoy the same activity and take pleasure in their company, either doing the activity together or discussing it.

Join a class. Singing is a rapid way to feel happier and closer to others. If you are not musical, other classes will also provide happiness boosts and a sense of greater connection with others.

Plan a group activity that will be enjoyable for others. It could be organising an outing or a meal. Any joy is likely to be amplified by doing it with others and you will become more popular with others by selfless acts.

EPILOGUE

I no longer indulge in the psychedelic drug-taking of my wanton youth. Today you are more likely to find me wandering around the fields of my beloved Somerset with my metal detector. Like many absorbing hobbies, metal-detecting is good for my mental well-being.[25] Whenever I feel the need to calm my mind, I go out detecting. It is a pastime that combines walking in nature, exercise, taking in the environment, focusing attention onto the sound of the detector, chatting to the occasional curious villager and, every so often, the promise of an interesting find. No wonder I find it so rewarding. There is even a recent Danish study that found detectorists regarded their hobby as having a significantly positive and lasting effect on their health and well-being.[26] Respondents reported that metal-detecting alleviated specific symptoms of their mental disorders, specifically depression and anxiety. However, the authors concluded that the main beneficial effect was deeply rooted in the interaction with archaeological heritage – a sense of connection with the past.

On my birthday this year, I uncovered an ancient coin in a field next to where I live that had been struck in Rome, over 1,200 miles away, and dated to around 170 AD. At the time, the nearby city of Aquae Sulis (modern Bath), with its natural hot springs, was the centre of decadence in Roman Britain. On one side of the coin was the head of Marcus Aurelius, the last of the five good emperors to rule during the height of the Roman Empire – he was the one portrayed by the Irish actor Richard Harris in the film *Gladiator*. Not only was he an emperor but he was also one of the Stoic philosophers who wrote about happiness. Marcus Aurelius was well aware of the perils of ego-centrism, as he is said to have hired an assistant to follow him around should anyone take the knee or praise him, whereupon the assistant was instructed to whisper into the emperor's ear, 'You're just a man. You're just a man.'

Marcus Aurelius coin. Rome Mint 170 AD.
(Permission: Author)

Epilogue

Marcus Aurelius's most famous quote is 'The happiness of your life depends on the quality of your thoughts.' Too true. Imagine my sheer joy and awe at holding in my hand a coin that was last touched by someone nearly 2,000 years ago. Who was that person? A Roman soldier? A local Briton? What would they have made of metal-detecting and all the wonders of the modern era? In that moment, considering the vastness of time and journey of our species, I felt an immense sense of contentment and connection with humanity, and this made me happy.

ACKNOWLEDGEMENTS

This book is the product of five years immersing myself in the field of positive psychology. This would not have been possible without a multitude of scientists who established the field, including Martin Seligman, Mihaly Csikszentmihalyi, Ed Diener, Dan Gilbert, Ed Wilson, Sonja Lyubomirsky, Barbara Fredrickson, Dacher Keltner and many, many more. I truly feel like an interloper when I consider the vast volume of work that has preceded me, but I do believe the developmental perspective I bring to the field is fresh and worthwhile.

I have dedicated this book to those who I have known and worked with for thirty years, but I would like to express my specific gratitude to Laurie Santos, who was responsible for the Science of Happiness course at Bristol and my colleague Sarah Jelbert, who joined me to help deliver the course after it was established. This course would not be the success it is without Laurie and Sarah, and I regard myself as very fortunate to be working with such great colleagues.

I am also enormously grateful to the University of Bristol, the

Elizabeth Blackwell Institute and in particular James Rowan, who have been so supportive in helping me deliver the Science of Happiness as well as Judith Squires, David Smith, Tansy Jessop, Paula Coonerty and the rest of the senior management.

Finally, I would like to thank my editor Assallah Tahir and assistant editor Sophia Akhtar for providing invaluable feedback on earlier drafts and reminding me that this is a book about happiness. Jaime Marshall is the energy and wisdom behind this book. I have known Jaime for many years as a friend and now as my agent, and 1 look forward to writing many more books together.

NOTES

Preface

1 Fisher, S. and Hood, B. (1987), The stress of the transition to university: A longitudinal study of psychological disturbance, absent-mindedness and vulnerability to homesickness, *British Journal of Psychology*, 78, pp. 425–441.

Introduction

1 Bartels, M. (2015), 'Genetics of wellbeing and its components satisfaction with life, happiness, and quality of life: a review and meta-analysis of heritability studies', *Behavioral Genetics*, 45(2), pp. 137–156.
2 Plomin, R. and von Stumm, S. (2018), 'The new genetics of intelligence', *Nature Reviews Genetics*, 19, pp. 148–59.
3 Office for National Statistics, 'Children's views on well-being and what makes a happy life, UK: 2020', https://www.ons.gov.uk/peoplepopulationandcommunity/wellbeing/articles/childrensviewsonwellbeingandwhatmakesahappylifeuk2020/2020-10-02 (accessed 26 September 2023)
4 Flèche, S., Lekfuangfu, W. N. and Clark, A. E. (2021), 'The long-lasting effects of family and childhood on adult wellbeing: evidence from British cohort data', *Journal of Economic Behavior and Organization*, 181, pp. 290–311.

5 Folk, D. and Dunn, E. (2023), 'A systematic review
   of the strength of evidence for the most commonly
   recommended happiness strategies in mainstream media',
   Nature Human Behaviour, https://doi.org/10.1038/s41562-
   023-01651-4 (accessed 26 September 2023). This recent
   review of studies recommending positive psychology
   intervention demonstrates that most have methodological
   weaknesses. That does not mean there is no evidence but,
   rather, they lack the rigorous evaluation that has recently
   become common practice, such as pre-registration and
   calculating adequate sample sizes. All of my research
   in this area has been pre-registered and checked for
   sampling biases.

6 Hood, B., Jelbert, S. and Santos, L. (2021), 'Benefits of a
   psychoeducational happiness course on university student
   mental well-being both before and during a Covid-19
   lockdown', *Health Psychology Open*, 8(1). Each run of the
   course has produced significant positive benefits every
   year by increasing well-being by about 10 per cent. That
   may not sound like much but that is the average for the
   group. Some students who really engaged with the course
   experienced much greater benefits. Also, who would not
   like to be 10 per cent smarter, wealthier or healthier?

7 Hobbs, C., Jelbert, S., Santos, L. R., and Hood, B. (in
   press), 'Long-term analysis of a psychoeducational
   course on university students' mental well-being,' *Higher
   Education*. Students who continued to use the techniques
   taught during the course maintained the benefits to
   happiness 1–2 years later.

Lesson One: Alter Your Ego

1 James, W. (1890), *Principles of Psychology* (New York: Holt)
2 Hood, B. (2012), *The Self Illusion* (London: Constable
   & Robinson)
3 Mascaro, J. (1973), *The Dhammapada* (London: Penguin)
4 Wearing, D. (2005), *Forever Today: A Memoir of Love and
   Amnesia* (London: Corgi)

5 Quoidbach, J., Gilbert, D. T. and Wilson T. D. (2013), 'The end of history illusion', *Science*, 339(6115), pp. 96–8.

6 Piaget, J. (1954), *The Construction of Reality in the Child* (London: Routledge)

7 Fantz, R. L. (1963), 'Pattern vision in newborn infants', *Science*, 140(3564), pp. 296–97.

8 Bushnell, I. W. R., Sai, F. and Mullin, J. T. (1989), 'Neonatal recognition of the mother's face', *British Journal of Developmental Psychology*, 7(1), pp. 3–15.

9 Adamson, L. B., Bakeman, R., Smith, C. B. et al. (1987), 'Adults' interpretation of infants' acts', *Developmental Psychology*, 23(3), pp. 383–87.

10 Hains, S. M. and Muir, D. W. (1996), 'Infant sensitivity to adult eye direction', *Child Development*, 67(5), pp. 1940–51.

11 Strathearn, Li, J., Fonagy, P. and Montague, R. (2008), 'What's in a smile? Maternal brain responses to infant facial cues', *Pediatrics*, 122(1), pp. 40–51.

12 Greenberg, D. J., Hillman, D. and Grice, D. (1973), 'Infant and stranger variables related to stranger anxiety in the first year of life', *Developmental Psychology*, 9(2), pp. 207–12.

13 Tarabulsy, G. M., Tessier, R. and Kappas, A. (1996), 'Contingency detection and the contingent organization of behavior in interactions: implications for socioemotional development in infancy', *Psychological Bulletin*, 120(1), pp. 25–41.

14 Watson, J. S. (2001), 'Contingency perception and misperception in infancy: some potential implications for attachment', *Bulletin of the Menninger Clinic*, 65(3), pp. 296–320.

15 Rennung, M. and Göritz, A. S. (2016), 'Prosocial consequences of interpersonal synchrony: a meta-analysis', *Zeitschrift fur Psychologie*, 224(3), pp. 168–89.

16 van Ijzendoorn, M. H., Schuengel, C., Wang, Q. et al. (2022), 'Improving parenting, child attachment, and externalizing behaviors: meta-analysis of the first 25 randomized controlled trials on the effects of Video-feedback intervention to promote Positive

Parenting and Sensitive Discipline', *Development and Psychopathology*, pp. 1–16.

17 Eacott, M. J. (1999), 'Memory for the events of early childhood', *Current Directions in Psychological Science*, 8(2), pp. 46–9.

18 Nadel, L. and Zola-Morgan, S. (1984), 'Infantile Amnesia' in M. Moscovitch (ed.), *Infant Memory – Advances in the Study of Communication and Affect*, Vol. 9 (Boston, MA: Springer)

19 Nelson, K. and Fivush, R. (2004), 'The emergence of autobiographical memory: a social cultural developmental theory', *Psychological Review*, 111(2), pp. 486–511.

20 Amsterdam, B. (1972), 'Mirror self-image reactions before age two', *Developmental Psychobiology*, 5(4), pp. 297–305.

21 Howe, M. L. and Courage, M. L. (1997), 'The emergence and early development of autobiographical memory', *Psychological Review*, 104(3), pp. 305–26.

22 Piaget, J. (1954), *The Construction of Reality in the Child* (New York: Basic Books)

23 Piaget, J., and Inhelder, B. (1956), *The Child's Conception of Space* (London: Routledge & Kegan Paul)

24 Flavell, J. H., Everett, B. A., Croft, K. et al. (1981), 'Young children's knowledge about visual perception: further evidence for the Level 1–Level 2 distinction', *Developmental Psychology*, 17(1), pp. 99–103.

25 Donaldson, M. (1978), *Children's Minds* (London: Fontana)

26 Gopnik, A. and Astington, J. W. (1988), 'Children's understanding of representational change and its relation to the understanding of false belief and the appearance-reality distinction', *Child Development*, 59(1), pp. 26–37.

27 Premack, D. and Woodruff, G. (1978), 'Does the chimpanzee have a theory of mind?', *Behavioral and Brain Sciences*, 1(4), pp. 515–26.

28 Harter, S. (1999), *The Construction of Self: A Developmental Perspective* (New York: Guilford Publications)

29 Fehr, E., Bernhard, H. and Rockenbach, B. (2008), 'Egalitarianism in young children', *Nature*, 454, pp. 1079–83.

Notes

30 Aboud, F. E. (2003), 'The formation of in-group favoritism and out-group prejudice in young children: Are they distinct attitudes?' *Developmental Psychology*, 39(1), pp. 48–60.

31 Harter, S. (2006), 'The Development of Self-Esteem' in M. H. Kernis (ed.), *Self-Esteem Issues and Answers: A Sourcebook of Current Perspectives* (New York: Psychology Press), pp. 144–50

32 Ibid.

33 Baumeister, R. F., Campbell, J. D., Krueger, J. I. et al. (2003), 'Does high self-esteem cause better performance, interpersonal success, happiness, or healthier lifestyles?', *Psychological Science in the Public Interest*, 4(1), pp. 1–44.

34 Baumrind, D. (1989), 'Rearing competent children,' in W. Damon (ed.), *Child Development Today and Tomorrow* (San Francisco: Jossey-Bass), pp. 349–73.

35 Litovsky, V. G. and Dusek, J. B. (1985), 'Perceptions of child rearing and self-concept development during the early adolescent years', *Journal of Youth and Adolescence*, 14(5), pp. 373–87.

36 Grolnick, W. and Ryan, R. (1989), 'Parent styles associated with children's self-regulation and competence in school', *Journal of Educational Psychology*, 81(2), pp. 143–54.

37 Maccoby, E. E. and Martin, J. A. (1983), 'Socialization in the context of the family' in E. M. Hetherington and P. H. Mussen (eds.), *Handbook of Child Psychology*, Vol. 4: *Socialization, Personality, and Social Development* (New York: Wiley), pp. 1–101.

38 Devine, R. T. and Hughes, C. (2014), 'Relations between false belief understanding and executive function in early childhood: a meta-analysis', *Child Development*, 85(5), pp. 1777–94.

39 Blair, R. J. R. (2012), 'Considering anger from a cognitive neuroscience perspective', *Wiley Interdisciplinary Reviews: Cognitive Science*, 3(1), pp. 165–74.

40 Blakemore, S.-J. (2018), *Inventing Ourselves: The Secret Life of the Teenage Brain* (London: Doubleday)

41 Cooley, C. H. (1902), *Human Nature and the Social Order* (New York: Scribner's).

42 Ware, B. (2012), *The Top Five Regrets of the Dying: A Life Transformed by the Dearly Departing* (London: Hay House).

Lesson Two: Avoid Isolation

1 Stearns, S. (1992), *The Evolution of Life Histories* (New York: Oxford University Press)

2 Gibbons, A. (2008), 'The birth of childhood', *Science*, 322(5904), pp. 1040–3.

3 Waldinger, R. and Shulz, M. (2023), *The Good Life: Lessons from the World's Longest Study on Happiness* (London: Rider)

4 Dunbar, R. I. M. (1998), 'The social brain hypothesis', *Evolutionary Anthropology*, 6(5), pp. 178–90.

5 Powel, J., Lewis, P. A., Roberts, N. et al. (2012), 'Orbital prefrontal cortex predicts social network size: an imaging study of individual differences in humans', *Proceedings of the Royal Society B: Biological Sciences*, 279(1736), pp. 2157–62.

6 Gavrilets, S. and Vose, A. (2006), 'The dynamics of Machiavellian intelligence', *Proceedings of the National Academy of Sciences*, 103(45), pp. 16823–8.

7 Tomasello, M., Kruger, A. and Ratner, H. (1993), 'Cultural learning', *Behavioral and Brain Sciences*, 16(3), pp. 495–552.

8 Isidro-Cloudas, Terri, 'Managing labor pain during childbirth', *Parents*, 20 July 2023, https://www.parents.com/pregnancy/giving-birth/labor-and-delivery/understanding-labor-pain/ (accessed 26 September 2023)

9 'Duration of Labor', Center for Academic Research & Training in Anthropogeny, https://carta.anthropogeny.org/moca/topics/duration-labor (accessed 4 March 2023)

10 Hawkes, K., O'Connell, J. F. and Blurton Jones, N. G. (1997), 'Hadza women's time allocation, offspring provisioning, and the evolution of postmenopausal life spans', *Current Anthropology*, 38(4), pp. 551–78.

11 Kim, P. S., Coxworth, J. E. and Hawkes, K. (2012), 'Increased longevity evolves from grandmothering,' *Proceedings of the Royal Society B*, 279(1749), pp. 4880–84.

12 de Waal, F. B. (2007), 'With a little help from a friend', *PLOS Biology*, 5(7), e190, https://doi.org/10.1371/journal.pbio.0050190 (accessed 8 November 2023)

13 Zhu, P., Liu, W., Zhang, X. et al. (2023), 'Correlated evolution of social organization and lifespan in mammals', *Nature Communications*, 14(1), p. 372.

14 Zeskind, P. S. and Lester, B. M. (2001), 'Analysis of infant crying' in L. T. Singer and P. S. Zeskind (eds.), *Biobehavioral Assessment of the Infant* (New York: Guilford), pp. 149–66

15 Hinde, R. (1982), 'Attachment: Some conceptual and biological issues' in C. M. Parkes and J. Stevenson-Hinde (eds.), *The Place of Attachment in Human Behavior* (New York: Basic Books), pp, 60–78.

16 Bowlby, J. (1953), *Child Care and the Growth of Love* (Baltimore: Pelican Books)

17 Harlow, H. (1958), 'The nature of love', *American Psychologist*, 13, pp. 573–685.

18 Suomi. S. J. and Harlow, H. (1972), 'Social rehabilitation in isolate-reared monkeys', *Developmental Psychology*, 6(3), pp. 487–96.

19 Rutter, M., O'Connor, T. G. and the English and Romanian Adoptees (ERA) Study Team (2004), 'Are there biological programming effects for psychological development? Findings from a study of Romanian adoptees', *Developmental Psychology*, 40(1), pp. 81–94.

20 Rutter, M., Colvert, E., Kreppner, J. et al. (2007), 'Early adolescent outcomes for institutionally-deprived and non-deprived adoptees. I: disinhibited attachment', *Journal of Child Psychology and Psychiatry*, 48(1), pp. 17–30.

21 Mackes, N. K., Golm, D., Sarkar, S. et al. (2020), 'Early childhood deprivation is associated with alterations in adult brain structure despite subsequent environmental enrichment', *PNAS*, 117(1), pp. 641–9.

22 Sonuga-Barke, E. J. S., Kennedy, M., Kumsta, R. et al. (2017), 'Child-to-adult neurodevelopmental and mental health trajectories after early life deprivation: the young adult follow-up of the longitudinal English and Romanian Adoptees study', *The Lancet*, 389(10078), pp. 1539–48.

23 Goodwin, M. H. (2002), 'Exclusion in girls' peer groups: ethnographic analysis of language practices on the playground', *Human Development*, 45(6), pp. 392–415.

24 van der Wal, Marcel F., de Wit, Cees A. M. and Hirasing, Remy A. (2003), 'Psychosocial health among young victims and offenders of direct and indirect bullying', *Pediatrics*, 111(6), pp. 1312–17.

25 Mandela, N. (1994), *Long Walk to Freedom* (London: Little Brown), p. 52.

26 Holte, A. J., Fisher, W. N. and Ferraro, F. R. (2022), 'Afraid of social exclusion: fear of missing out predicts Cyberball-induced ostracism', *Journal of Technology in Behavioral Science*, 7(3), pp. 315–24.

27 Williams, K. D. and Jarvis, B. (2006), 'Cyberball: a program for use in research on ostracism and interpersonal acceptance', *Behavior Research Methods*, 38(1), pp. 174–80.

28 Hartgerink, C. H. J., van Beest, I., Wicherts, J. M. et al. (2015), 'The ordinal effects of ostracism: a meta-analysis of 120 Cyberball studies', *PLOS ONE*, 10(5), e0127002, https://doi.org/10.1371/journal.pone.0127002 (accessed 8 November 2023)

29 Williams, K. D. (2007), 'Ostracism: the kiss of social death', *Social and Personality Psychology Compass*, 1(1), pp. 236–47.

30 Eisenberger, N. I., Lieberman, M. D. and Williams, K. D. (2003), 'Does rejection hurt? An fMRI study of social exclusion', *Science*, 302(5643), pp. 290–2.

31 Holt-Lunstad, J. and Clark, B. D. (2014), 'Social stressors and cardiovascular response: influence of ambivalent relationships and behavioral ambivalence', *International Journal of Psychophysiology*, 93(3), pp. 381–9.

32 Duscheck, S., Nassauer, L. et. al. (2020), 'Dispositional empathy is associated with experimental pain reduction during provision of social support by romantic partners', *Scandinavian Journal of Pain*, 20(1), pp. 205–9.

33 Holt-Lunstad, J., Smith, T. B., Baker, M. et al. (2015), 'Loneliness and social isolation as risk factors for mortality: a meta-analytic review', *Perspectives in Psychological Science*, 10(2), pp. 227–37.

34 US Department of Health and Human Services, 'New Surgeon General advisory raises alarm about the devastating impact of the epidemic of loneliness and isolation in the United States', 3 May 2023, https://www.hhs.gov/about/news/2023/05/03/new-surgeon-general-advisory-raises-alarm-about-devastating-impact-epidemic-loneliness-isolation-united-states.html (accessed 26 September 2023)

35 Cigna Group (2021), 'The loneliness epidemic persists: a post-pandemic look at the state of loneliness among US adults', https://newsroom.thecignagroup.com/loneliness-epidemic-persists-post-pandemic-look (accessed 26 September 2023)

36 Holt-Lunstad, J., Smith, T. B. and Layton, B. (2010), 'Social relationships and mortality risk: a meta-analytic review', *PLOS Medicine*, 7(7), e1000316, https://doi.org/10.1371/journal.pmed.1000316 (accessed 27 September 2023)

37 Hayward, C., Killen, J. D., Kraemer, H. C. et al. (1998), 'Linking self-reported childhood behavioral inhibition to adolescent social phobia', *Journal of the American Academy of Child and Adolescent Psychiatry*, 37(12), pp. 1308–16.

38 Morey, J. N., Boggero, I. A., Scott, A.B. et al. (2015), 'Current directions in stress and human immune function', *Current Opinion in Psychology*, 5, pp. 13–17.

39 Kross, K. J. and Gunnar, M. R. (2018), 'Early adversity, the HPA axis, and child psychopathology', *Journal of Child Psychology and Psychiatry*, 59(4), pp. 327–46.

40 Yehuda, R. Engel, S. M., Brand, S. R., et al. (2005), 'Transgenerational effects of posttraumatic stress disorder

in babies of mothers exposed to the World Trade Center attacks during pregnancy', *Journal of Clinical Endocrinology & Metabolism*, 90(7), pp. 4115–8.

41 Kahneman, D. (2012), *Thinking, Fast and Slow*, (London: Penguin)

42 Yu, S. (2016), 'Stress potentiates decision biases: a stress induced deliberation-to-intuition (SIDI) model', *Neurobiology of Stress*, 3, pp. 83–95.

43 Gross, A., 'Survey says: men are more aggressive behind the wheel,' *AAA News Room*, 12 March 2020, https://newsroom.aaa.com/2020/12/survey-says-men-are-more-aggressive-behind-the-wheel/ (accessed 16 March 2023)

44 Petrova, D., Garcia-Retamero, R. and Catena, A. (2015), 'Lonely hearts don't get checked: on the primary role of social support in screening for cardiovascular disease', *Preventive Medicine*, 81, pp. 202–8.

45 Mendonça G., Cheng L. A., Mélo, E. N. et al. (2014), 'Physical activity and social support in adolescents: a systematic review', *Health Education Research*, 29(5), pp. 822–39.

46 'Charities Aid Foundation UK Giving Report 2021' (2021), Charities Aid Foundation, https://www.cafonline.org/docs/default-source/about-us-research/uk_giving_report_2021.pdf (accessed 8 November 2023)

47 Hadero, Haleluya and the Associated Press, 'Americans gave a record $471 billion to charity in 2020', *Fortune*, 15 June 2021, https://fortune.com/2021/06/15/americans-gave-a-record-471-billion-to-charity-in-2020-pandemic/ (accessed 26 September 2023)

48 Fisher, R. A. (1930), *The Genetical Theory of Natural Selection* (Oxford: Clarendon Press)

49 Trivers, R. L. (1971), 'The evolution of reciprocal altruism', *Quarterly Review of Biology*, 46(1), pp. 35–57.

50 Carter, G. G. and Wilkinson, G. S. (2015), 'Social benefits of non-kin food sharing by female vampire bats', https://doi.org/10.1098/rspb.2015.2524 (accessed 26 September 2023)

Notes

51 Smith, S., Windmeijer, F. and Wright, E. (2013), 'Peer effects in charitable giving: evidence from the (running) field', *Economic Journal,* 125(585), pp. 1053–71.

52 Camerer, C. F. (2003), *Behavioral Game Theory: Experiments in Strategic Interaction* (Princeton, NJ: Princeton University Press)

53 Bardsley, N. (2008), 'Dictator game giving: altruism or artefact?', *Experimental Economics,* 11(2), pp. 122–33.

54 *Friends,* Series 5, Episode 4: 'The One Where Phoebe Hates PBS', first broadcast on NBC 15 October 1998.

55 Dunn, E. W., Aknin, L. B. and Norton, M. I. (2008), 'Spending money on others promotes happiness', *Science,* 319(5870), pp. 1687–8.

56 Andreoni, J. (1990), 'Impure altruism and donations to public goods: a theory of warm-glow giving', *Economic Journal,* 100(401), pp. 464–77.

57 Aknin, L. B. et al. (2013), 'Prosocial spending and well-being: cross-cultural evidence for a psychological universal', *Journal of Personality and Social Psychology,* 104(4), pp. 635–52.

58 Park, S. Q. et al. (2017), 'A neural link between generosity and happiness', *Nature Communications,* 8, doi: 10.1038/ncomms15964 (accessed 26 September 2023)

59 Wilson, T. D., Centerbar, D. B., Kermer, D. A. et al. (2005), 'The pleasures of uncertainty: prolonging positive moods in ways people do not anticipate', *Journal of Personality and Social Psychology,* 88(1), pp. 5–21.

60 Kemp, S. (2024). The Time We Spend on Social Media, https://datareportal.com/reports/digital-2024-deep-dive-the-time-we-spend-on-social-media.

61 Thierer, A. (2009), 'Against Techno-Panics', Scribd, https://www.scribd.com/document/17392730/Against-Techno-Panics-by-Adam-Thierer-PFF-July-2009-Inside-ALEC (accessed 5 March 2023)

62 Festinger, L. (1954), 'A theory of social comparison processes', *Human Relations,* 7(2), pp. 117–40.

63 Vogel, E. A., Rose, J. P., Okdie, B. M. et al. (2015), 'Who

compares and despairs? The effect of social comparison orientation on social media use and its outcomes', *Personality and Individual Differences*, 86, pp. 249–56.

64 Appel, M., Marker, C. and Gnambs, T. (2020), 'Are social media ruining our lives? A review of meta- analytic evidence', *Review of General Psychology*, 24(1), pp. 60–74.

65 Haidt, J. (2024). *The Anxious Generation: How the Great Rewiring of Childhood Is Causing an Epidemic of Mental Illness.* (London: Allen Lane)

66. Monteith, S., Glenn, T., Geddes J. R., Whybrow, P. C., Achtyes, E. D., Bauer, M. (2024). 'Implications of Online Self-Diagnosis in Psychiatry', *Pharmacopsychiatry*, 202457(2):45–52. doi: 10.1055/a-2268-5441.

67. Foulkes, L. & Andrews, J. L. (2023). 'Are mental health awareness efforts contributing to the rise in reported mental health problems? A call to test the prevalence inflation hypothesis', *New Ideas in Psychology*, 69, 101010.

68 Orben, A., Meier, A., Dalgleish & Blakemore, S-J (2024). 'Mechanisms linking social media use to adolescent mental health vulnerability.' *Nature Reviews Psychology*, https://doi.org/10.1038/s44159-024-00307-y (Accessed July 2024)

Lesson Three: Reject Negative Comparisons

1 Schacter, D., Gilbert, D., Wegner, D. et al. (2019), *Psychology* (London: Red Globe Press)

2 Tversky, A. and Kahneman, D. (1974), 'Judgment under uncertainty: heuristics and biases', *Science*, 185(4157), pp. 1124–31.

3 Pendry, L. F., Driscoll, D. M. and Field, S. C. T. (2007), 'Diversity training: putting theory into practice', *Journal of Occupational and Organizational Psychology*, 80(1), pp. 27–50.

4 Kahneman, D. (2012), *Thinking, Fast and Slow* (London: Penguin)

5 Medvec, V., Madey, S. F. and Gilovich, T. (1995), 'When less is more: counterfactual thinking and satisfaction among Olympic medalists', *Journal of Personality and Social Psychology*, 69(4), 603–10.

6 Triplett, N. (1898), 'The dynamogenic factors in pacemaking and competition', *American Journal of Psychology*, 9(4), pp. 507–33.

7 Baumeister, R. F. (1984), 'Choking under pressure: self consciousness and paradoxical effects of incentives on skilful performance', *Journal of Personality and Social Psychology*, 46(3), pp. 610–20.

8 Taylor, S.E. and Brown, J. (1988), 'Illusion and wellbeing: a social psychological perspective on mental health', *Psychological Bulletin*, 103(2), pp. 193–210.

9 Kahn, V. (2022), 'Survey says: appreciation matters more than you think', Bonusly, 2 March 2022, https:// blog.bonus.ly/ employee- appreciation- survey (accessed 5 February 2023)

10 Solnick, S. J. and Hemenway, D. (1998), 'Is more always better? A survey on positional concerns', *Journal of Economic Behavior & Organization*, 37(3), pp. 373–83.

11 Frank, R. (1993), *Choosing the Right Pond: Human Behavior and the Quest for Status* (New York: OUP USA)

12 Smith, D., 'Most people have no idea whether they're paid fairly', *Harvard Business Review*, December 2015, https:// hbr.org/2015/10/most- people- have- no- idea- whethertheyre- paid- fairly (accessed 5 February 2023)

13 Clark, A. E. (2003), 'Unemployment as a social norm: psychological evidence from panel data', *Journal of Labor Economics*, 21(2), pp. 289–322.

14 Hetschko, C., Knabe, A. and Schob, R. (2014), 'Changing identity: retiring from unemployment', *Economic Journal*, 124(575), pp. 149–66.

15 'Public opinions and social trends, Great Britain: 27 April to 8 May 2022', https://www.ons.gov. uk/ peoplepopulationandcommunity/wellbeing/ bulletins/ publicopinionsandsocialtrendsgreatbritain/ 27aprilto8may2022 (accessed 5 February 2023)

16 Deri, S., Davidai, S. and Gilovich, T. (2017), 'Home alone: why people believe others' social lives are richer than their own', *Journal of Personality and Social Psychology*, 113(6), pp. 858–77.

17 Brickman, P. and Campbell, D. T. (1971), 'Hedonic relativism and planning the good society' in M. H. Apley (ed.), *Adaptation Level Theory: A Symposium* (New York: Academic Press)

18 Brickman P., Coates, D. and Janoff-Bulman, R. (1978), 'Lottery winners and accident victims – is happiness relative?', *Journal of Personality and Social Psychology*, 36(8), pp. 917–27.

19 Lindqvist, E., Östling, R. and Cesarini, D. (2020), 'Long-run effects of lottery wealth on psychological well-being', *Review of Economic Studies*, 87(6), pp. 2703–26.

20 Duggan, C., Wilson, C., DiPonio, L. et al. (2016), 'Resilience and happiness after spinal cord injury: a qualitative study', *Topics in Spinal Cord Injury Rehabilitation*, 22(2), pp. 99–110.

21 Sackett, D. L. and Torrance, G. W. (1978), 'The utility of different health states as perceived by the general public', *Journal of Chronic Diseases*, 31(11), pp. 697–704.

22 Gilbert, D. (2006), *Stumbling on Happiness* (London: Harper Perennial)

23 Gilbert, D. and Wilson, T. (2003), 'Affective forecasting', *Advances in Experimental Social Psychology*, 35, pp. 345–411.

24 Levine, L. J., Lench, H. C., Kaplan, R. L. et al. (2012), 'Accuracy and artifact: reexamining the intensity bias in affective forecasting', *Journal of Personality and Social Psychology*, 103(4), pp. 584–605.

25 Ayton, P., Pott, A. and Elwakili, N. (2007), 'Affective forecasting: why can't people predict their emotions?', *Thinking & Reasoning*, 13(1), pp. 62–80.

26 Amornsiripanitch, N., Gompiners, P., Hu, G. et al. (2022), 'Failing just fine: assessing careers of venture capital-backed entrepreneurs via a non-wage measure', working paper 30179, National Bureau of Economic Research, doi 10.3386/w30179 (accessed 26 September 2023)

27 Wilson, T., Wheatley, T. P., Myers, J. M. et al. (2000), 'Focalism: a source of durability bias in affective forecasting', *Journal of Personality and Social Psychology*, 78(5), pp. 821–36.

28 Ubel, P. A., Loewenstein, G. and Jepson, C. (2003), 'Whose quality of life? A commentary exploring discrepancies between health state evaluations of patients

and the general public', *Quality of Life Research,* 12(6), pp. 599–607.

29 Apouey, B. and Clark, A. E (2015), 'Winning big but feeling no better? The effect of lottery prizes on physical and mental health', *Health Economics,* 24(5), pp. 516–38.

30 Kuhn, P., Kooreman, P. and Soetevent, A. (2011), 'The effects of lottery prizes on winners and their neighbors: evidence from the Dutch postcode lottery', *American Economic Review,* 101(5), pp. 2226–47.

31 Doll, J., 'A treasury of terribly sad stories of lotto winners', *The Atlantic,* 30 March 2012, https://www.theatlantic.com/national/archive/2012/03/terribly-sad-true-stories-lotto-winners/329903/ (accessed 5 February 2023)

32 Strack, F., Martin, L. and Schwarz, N. (1988), 'Priming and communication: social determinants of information use in judgments of life satisfaction', *European Journal of Social Psychology,* 18(5), pp. 429–42.

33 Ferster, C. B. and Skinner, B. F. (1957), *Schedules of Reinforcement* (New York: Appleton-Century-Crofts)

34 Olds, J. and Milner, P. (1954), 'Positive reinforcement produced by electrical stimulation of the septal area and other regions of rat brain', *Journal of Comparative Physiology and Psychology,* 47(6), pp. 419–27.

35 Olds J. (1956), 'Pleasure centers in the brain', *Scientific American,* 1 October 1956, https://www.scientificamerican.com/article/pleasure-centers-in-the-brain/ (accessed 8 November 2023)

36 Dunlop, B. W. and Nemeroff, C. B. (2007), 'The role of dopamine in the pathophysiology of depression', *Archives of General Psychiatry,* 64(3), pp. 327–37.

37 Wise, R.A. (2008). 'Dopamine and reward: the anhedonia hypothesis 30 years on', *Neurotoxity Research,* 14, pp. 169–83.

38 Cannon, C. M. and Palmiter, R. D. (2003), 'Reward without dopamine', *Journal of Neuroscience,* 23(34), pp. 10827–31.

39 Heath, R. G. (1972), 'Pleasure and brain activity in man', *Journal of Nervous and Mental Disease*, 154(1), pp. 3–18.

40 Bell, V., 'The unsexy truth about dopamine', *The Guardian*, 3 February 2013.

41 Chase, H. W. and Clark, L. (2010), 'Gambling severity predicts midbrain response to near-miss outcomes', *Journal of Neuroscience*, 30(18), pp. 6180–7.

42 Odum, A.L. (2011), 'Delay discounting: I'm a K, you're a K', *Journal of the Experimental Analysis of Behavior*, 96(3), pp. 427–39.

43 Gilbert, D. T. and Wilson, T. D. (2000), 'Miswanting: some problems in the forecasting of future affective states', in J. P. Forgas (ed.), *Feeling and Thinking: The Role of Affect in Social Cognition* (Cambridge: Cambridge University Press), pp. 178–97.

44 Schwartz, B., 'The tyranny of choice', *Scientific American*, 1 December 2004, https://www.scientificamerican.com/article/the-tyranny-of-choice/ (accessed 8 November 2023)

45 Schwartz, B., Ward, A., Monterosso, J., Lyubomirsky, S., White. K., and Lehman, D. R. (2002), 'Maximizing versus satisficing: happiness is a matter of choice', *Journal of Personality and Social Psychology*, 83(5), pp. 1178–97.

Lesson Four: Become More Optimistic

1 Dahlgreen, W., 'Chinese people are most likely to feel the world is getting better', YouGov US, 5 January 2016, https://yougov.co.uk/topics/society/articles-reports/2016/01/05/chinese-people-are-most-optimistic-world (accessed 16 March 2023)

2 Pinker, S. (2018), *Enlightenment Now: The Case for Reason, Science, Humanism and Progress* (London: Penguin)

3 Gallagher, M. W., Lopez, S. J. and Pressman, S. D. (2013), 'Optimism is universal: exploring the presence and benefits of optimism in a representative sample of the world', *Journal of Personality*, 81(5), pp. 429–40.

4 Sharot, T. (2012), *The Optimism Bias: Why We're Wired to Look on the Bright Side* (London: Robinson)

5 Barnes, H., 'Why big law firms' attorneys are so likely to get divorced: stressed, tired, mad and with nothing more to give', https://www.bcgsearch.com/article/900049580/Why-Big-Firm-Attorneys-Are-So-Likely-to-Get-Divorced/ (accessed 17 March 2023)

6 Rasmussen, H. N., Scheier, M. F. and Greenhouse, J. B. (2009), 'Optimism and physical health: a meta-analytic review', *Annals of Behavioral Medicine*, 37(3), pp. 239–56.

7 Baumeister, R. F., Bratslavsky, E., Finkenauer, C. et al. (2001), 'Bad is stronger than good', *Review of General Psychology*, 5(4), pp. 323–70; see also Rozin, O. and Royzman, E. B. (2001), 'Negativity bias, negativity dominance and contagion', *Personality and Social Psychology Review*, 5(4), pp. 296–320.

8 Fox, E., Lester, V., Russo, R. et al (2000), 'Facial expressions of emotion: are angry faces detected more efficiently?', *Cognition and Emotion*, 14(1), pp. 61–92.

9 Burra, N., Kerzel, D., Muniz, D. et al. (2018), 'Early spatial attention deployment toward and away from aggressive voices', *Social Cognitive and Affective Neuroscience*, 14(1), pp. 73–80.

10 Zhao, C., Chronaki, G., Schiessl, I. et al. (2019), 'Is infant neural sensitivity to vocal emotion associated with mother-infant relational experience?', *PLOS ONE*, 14(2), e0212205, https://doi.org/10.1371/journal.pone.0212205 (accessed 27 September 2023)

11 Mumme, D. L., Fernald, A., Herrera, C. (1996), 'Infants' responses to facial and vocal emotional signals in a social referencing paradigm', *Child Development*, 67(6), pp. 3219–37.

12 Hornik, R., Risenhoover, N. and Gunnar, M. (1987), 'The effects of maternal positive, neutral, and negative affective communications on infant responses to new toys', *Child Development*, 58(4), pp. 937–44.

13 Anderson, E. C., Carleton, R. N., Diefenbach, M. et

al. (2019), 'The relationship between uncertainty and affect', *Frontiers in Psychology*, 10, 2504, https://doi.org/10.3389/fpsyg.2019.02504 (accessed 27 September 2023)

14 Sharot, T., Martorella, E. A., Delgado, M. R. et al. (2007), 'How personal experience modulates the neural circuitry of memories of September 11', *PNAS*, 104(1), pp. 389–94.

15 Gilbert, D. T., Pinel, E. C., Wilson, T. D. et al. (1998), 'Immune neglect: a source of durability bias in affective forecasting', *Journal of Personality and Social Psychology*, 75(3), pp. 617–38.

16 Tierney, J. and Baumeister, R. F. (2019), *The Power of Bad: And How to Overcome It* (London: Allen Lane), p. 11.

17 Schopenhauer, A. (1958), *The World as Will and Representation*, trans. E. F. J. Payne (Indian Hills, Colorado: The Falcon's Wing Press)

18 de Hoog, N. and Verboon, P. (2020), 'Is the news making us unhappy? The influence of daily news exposure on emotional states', *British Journal of Psychology*, 111(2), pp. 157–73.

19 Price, M., Legrand, A. C., Brier, Z. M. F. et al. (2022), 'Doomscrolling during COVID-19: the negative association between daily social and traditional media consumption and mental health symptoms during the COVID-19 pandemic', *Psychological Trauma: Theory, Research, Practice, Policy*, 14(8), pp. 1338–46.

20 Taher, A. and Perthen, A., 'Meat cattle slaughtered in "cruel" kosher method is in your high street burger', Mail Online, 16 March 2014, https://www.dailymail.co.uk/news/article-2581918/meat-cattle-slaughtered-cruel-kosher-ceremony-high-street-burger.html (accessed 27 September 2023)

21 Willis, J. and Todorov, A. (2006), 'First impressions: making up your mind after 100ms exposure to a face', *Psychological Science*, 17(7), pp. 592–8.

22 Ferguson, M. J., Mann, T. C., Cone, J. et al. (2019), 'When and how implicit first impressions can be

updated', *Current Directions in Psychological Science*, 28(4), pp. 331–6.

23 Riskey, D. R. and Birnbaum, M. H. (1974), 'Compensatory effects in moral judgement: Two rights don't make up for a wrong', *Journal of Experimental Psychology*, 103(1), pp. 171–3.

24 Klein, N. and O'Brien, E. (2016), 'The tipping point of moral change: when do good and bad acts make good and bad actors?', *Social Cognition*, 34(2), pp. 149–66.

25 Gottman, J. (1994), *Why Marriages Succeed or Fail* (New York: Simon & Schuster)

26 Ross, L. (1977), 'The intuitive psychologists and his shortcomings' in L. Berkowitz (ed.), *Advances in Experimental Social Psychology*, Vol. 10. (New York: Academic Press)

27 Learner, M. J. (1980), *The Belief in a Just World: A Fundamental Delusion* (New York: Plenum Press)

28 Averill, J. R. (1973), 'Personal control over aversive stimuli and its relationship to stress', Psychological Bulletin, **80**, pp. 286–303.

29 Weisenberg, M., Wolf. Y., Mittwoch T., et al. (1985), 'Subject versus experimenter control in the reaction to pain', *Pain*, 23(2), pp. 187–200.

30 Arntz A. and Schmidt, A. J. M. (1989), 'Perceived control and the experience of pain' in A. Steptoe and A. Appels (eds.), *Stress, Personal Control and Health* (Brussels: Wiley), pp. 131–62.

31 Seligman, M. E. (1972), 'Learned helplessness', *Annual Review of Medicine*, 23, pp. 407–12.

32 Abramson, L., Seligman, M. E. and Teasdale, J. D. (1978), 'Learned helplessness in humans: critique and reformulation', *Journal of Abnormal Psychology*, 87(1), pp. 49–74.

33 Bates, T. C. (2015), 'The glass is half full and half empty: a population-representative twin study testing if optimism and pessimism are distinct systems', *Journal of Positive Psychology,* 10(6), pp. 533–42.

34 Plomin, R., Scheier, M. F., Bergeman, C. S. et al. (1992), 'Optimism, pessimism and mental health: a twin/ adoption analysis', *Personality and Individual Differences*, 13(8), pp. 921–30.

35 Heinonen, K., Räikkönen, K., Matthews K. A. et al. (2006), 'Socioeconomic status in childhood and adulthood: associations with dispositional optimism and pessimism over a 21-year follow-up', *Journal of Personality*, 74(4), pp. 1111–26.

36 Ek, E., Remes, J. and Sovio, U. (2004), 'Social and developmental predictors of optimism from infancy to early adulthood', *Social Indicators Research*, 69(2), pp. 219–42.

37 Petersen, C., Semmel, A., von Baeyer, C. et al. (1982), 'The attributional styles questionnaire', *Cognitive Therapy and Research*, 6, pp. 287–300.

38 Seligman, M. E. P. (2006), *Learned Optimism: How to Change Your Mind and Your Life* (New York: Vintage Books)

39 Malouff, J. M. and Schutte, N. S. (2017), 'Can psychological interventions increase optimism? A meta-analysis', *Journal of Positive Psychology*, 12(6), pp. 594–604.

40 Lee, L. O., James, P., Zevon, E. S. et al. (2019), 'Optimism is associated with exceptional longevity in 2 epidemiologic cohorts of men and women', *Proceedings of the National Academy of Sciences*, 116(37), pp. 18357–62.

41 Bruininks, P. and Malle, B. F. (2005), 'Distinguishing hope from optimism and related affective states', *Motivation and Emotion*, 29(4), pp. 324–52.

42 Sheier, M. F. and Carver, C. S. (2018), 'Dispositional optimism and physical health: a long look back, a quick look forward', *American Psychologist*, 73(9), pp. 1082–94.

43 Segerstrom, S. C. (2001), 'Optimism, goal conflict and stressor-related immune change', *Journal of Behavioral Medicine*, 24(5), pp. 441–67.

44 Andersson, M. A. (2012), 'Dispositional optimism and the emergence of social network diversity', Sociological Quarterly, 53(1), pp. 92–115.

45 Rius-Ottenheim, N., Kromhout, D., van der Mast, R. C. et al. (2012), 'Dispositional optimism and loneliness in older men', *International Journal of Geriatric Psychiatry*, 27(2), pp. 151–9.

46 Cross, A. and Sheffield, D. (2019), 'Mental contrasting for health behaviour change: a systematic review and meta-analysis of effects and moderator variables', *Health Psychology Review*, 13(2), pp. 209–25.

47 Oettingen, G. and Gollwitzer, P. M. (2004), 'Goal setting and goal striving' in M. B. Brewer and M. Hewstone (eds.), *Emotion and Motivation* (Oxford: Blackwell Publishing), pp. 165–83.

48 https://www.woopmylife.org (accessed 27 September 2023)

49 Stadler, G., Oettingen, G. and Gollwitzer, P. M. (2010), 'Intervention effects of information and self-regulation on eating fruits and vegetables over two years', *Health Psychology*, 29(3), pp. 274–83.

Lesson Five: Control Your Attention

1 James, W. (1890), *The Principles of Psychology* (Cambridge, MA: Harvard University Press)

2 Klinger, E. (1978), 'Modes of normal conscious flow' in K. S. Pope and J. L. Singer (eds.), *The Stream of Consciousness* (New York: Plenum), pp. 225–58.

3 Smallwood, J., Schooler, J. W., Turk, D. et al. (2011), 'Self-reflection and the temporal focus of the wandering mind', *Consciousness and Cognition*, 20(4), pp. 1120–26.

4 Atance, C. (2008), 'Future thinking in young children', *Current Directions in Psychological Science*, 17(4), pp. 295–8.

5 Busby, J. and Suddendorf, T. (2005), 'Recalling yesterday and predicting tomorrow', *Cognitive Development*, 20(3), pp. 362–72.

6 Howe, M. L. and Courage, M. L. (1997), 'The emergence and early development of autobiographical memory', *Psychological Review*, 104(3), pp. 499–523.

7 McCormack, T., Burns, P., O'Connor, P. et al. (2019), 'Do children and adolescents have a future-oriented bias? A

developmental study of spontaneous and cued past and future thinking', *Psychological Research*, 83(4), pp. 774–87.

8 Clark, S. H. (1996), 'The development of leisure in Britain, 1700-1850', Victorian Web, https://victorianweb.org/history/leisure1.html (accessed 27 September 2023)

9 Ortiz-Ospina, E., Giattino, C. and Roser, M. (2020), 'Time use', Our World in Data, https://ourworldindata.org/time-use (accessed 11 March 2023)

10 Killingsworth, M. and Gilbert, D. (2010), 'A wandering mind is an unhappy mind', *Science*, 330(6006), p. 932.

11 Kane, M. J., Brown, L. H., McVay, J. C. et al. (2007), 'For whom the mind wanders, and when: an experience-sampling study of working memory and executive control in daily life', *Psychological Science*, 18(7), pp. 614–21.

12 Smallwood J. and O'Connor, R. C. (2011), 'Imprisoned by the past: unhappy moods lead to a retrospective bias to mind wandering', *Cognition and Emotion*, 25(8), pp. 1481–90.

13 Raichle, M. (2015), 'The brain's default mode network', *Annual Review of Neuroscience*, 8(38), pp. 433–47.

14 Johnson, S. C., Baxter, L. C., Wilder, L. S. et al. (2002), 'Neural correlates of self-reflection', *Brain*, 125(8), pp. 1808–14.

15 Gallagher, H. L., Jack, A. I., Roepstorff, A. et al. (2002), 'Imaging the intentional stance in a competitive game', *Neuroimage*, 16(3, pt.1), pp. 814–21.

16 Hamilton, J. P., Farmer, M., Fogelman, P. et al. (2015), 'Depressive rumination, the default-mode network, and the dark matter of clinical neuroscience', *Biological Psychiatry*, 78(4), pp. 224–30.

17 Spreng, R. N., Dimas, E., Mwilambwe-Tshilobo, L. et al. (2020), 'The default network of the human brain is associated with perceived social isolation', *Nature Communications*, 11, article 6393, https://www.nature.com/articles/s41467-020-20039-w (accessed 27 September 2023)

18 Wilson, E. O. (1984), *Biophilia* (Cambridge, MA: Harvard University Press)

Notes

19 MacKerron, G. and Mourato, S. (2001), 'Fears, phobias, and preparedness: toward an evolved module of fear and fear learning', *Psychological Review*, 108(3), pp. 483–522.

20 Weinstein, N., Balmford, A., DeHaan, C. R. et al. (2015), 'Seeing community for the trees: the links among contact with natural environments, community cohesion, and crime', *Bioscience*, 65(12), pp. 1141–53.

21 Gaekwad, J. S., Sal Moslehian, A., Roös, P. B. et al. (2022), 'A meta-analysis of emotional evidence for the biophilia hypothesis and implications for biophilic design', *Frontiers in Psychology*, 13, article 750245, https://doi.org/10.3389/fpsyg.2022.750245 (accessed 27 September 2023)

22 Most published studies on the benefits of natural environments do not conform to the most rigorous standards for research publication. See Folk, D. and Dunn, E. (2023), 'A systematic review of the strength of evidence for the most commonly recommended happiness strategies in mainstream media', *Nature Human Behaviour*, https://doi.org/10.1038/s41562-023-01651-4 (accessed 27 September 2023). This does not mean that there is no evidence to support the benefits of walking in nature but, rather, the studies were not pre-registered and were underpowered.

23 Park, B. J., Tsunetsugu, Y., Kasetani, T. et al. (2010), 'The physiological effects of *Shinrin-yoku* (taking in the forest atmosphere or forest bathing): evidence from field experiments in 24 forests across Japan', *Environmental Health and Preventive Medicine*, 15, pp. 18–26.

24 Ulrich, R. S., Simons, R. F., Losito, B. D. et al. (1991), 'Stress recovery during exposure to natural and urban environments', *Journal of Environmental Psychology*, 11(3), pp. 201–30.

25 Amsel, L., Harbo, S. and Halberstam, A. (2015), 'There is nothing to fear but the amygdala: applying advances in the neuropsychiatry of fear to public policy', *Mind & Society*, 14, pp. 141–52.

26 Lederbogen, F., Kirsch, P., Haddad, L. et al. (2011), 'City

living and urban upbringing affect neural social stress processing in humans', *Nature*, 474(7352), pp. 498–501.

27 Sudiman, S., Sale, V. and Kühn, S. (2022), 'How nature nurtures: amygdala activity decreases as the result of a one-hour walk in nature', *Molecular Psychiatry*, 27(11), pp. 4446–52.

28 White, M. P., Alcock, I., Grellier, J. et al. (2019), 'Spending at least 120 minutes a week in nature is associated with good health and wellbeing', *Scientific Reports*, 9(1), article 7730, doi.org/10.1038/s41598-019-44097-3 (accessed 8 November 2023)

29 Tester-Jones, M., White, M. P., Elliot, L. R. et al. (2020), 'Results from an 18 country cross-sectional study examining experiences of nature for people with common mental health disorders', *Scientific Reports*, 10(1), article 19408, https://doi.org/10.1038/s41598-020-75825-9 (accessed 8 November 2023)

30 Bratman, G. N., Hamilton, J. P., Hahjn, K. S. et al. (2015), 'Nature experience reduces rumination and subgenual prefrontal cortex activation', *Proceedings of the National Academy of Sciences*, 112(28), pp. 8567–72.

31 Bratman, G. N., Daily, G. C., Levy, B. J. et al. (2015), 'The benefits of nature experience: improved affect and cognition', *Landscape and Urban Planning*, 138, pp. 41–50.

32 Ohly, H., White, M. P., Wheeler, B. W. et al. (2016), 'Attention restoration theory: a systematic review of the attention restoration potential of exposure to natural environments', *Journal of Toxicology and Environmental Health*, 19(7), pp. 305–43.

33 Bladwin, C. L., Roberts, D. M. and Barragan, D. (2017), 'Detecting and quantifying mind wandering during simulated driving', *Frontiers in Human Neuroscience*, 11, https://doi.org/10.3389/fnhum.2017.00406 (accessed 27 September 2023)

34 Wegner, D. M. (1994), 'Ironic processes of mental control', *Psychological Review*, 101(1), pp. 34–52.

35 Wegner, D. M. (1994), *White Bears and Other Unwanted*

Notes

Thoughts: Suppression, Obsession, and the Psychology of Mental Control (New York: Guilford Press)

36 Wegner, D. (1997), 'Why the mind wanders', in J. D. Cohen and J. W. Schooler (eds.), *Scientific Approaches to Consciousness* (Mahwah, NJ: Erlbaum), p. 304.

37 Goyal, M. (2014), 'Meditation programs for psychological stress and well-being. A systematic review and meta-analysis', *JAMA Internal Medicine*, 174, 357–68.

38 Jonides, J. (1981), 'Voluntary versus automatic control over the mind's eye's movement', in J. B. Long and A. D. Baddeley (eds.), *Attention & Performance,* Vol. 4 (New Jersey: Erlbaum), pp. 187–203.

39 Wegner, D. M., Schneider, D. J., Carter, S. et al. (1987), 'Paradoxical effects of thought suppression', *Journal of Personality and Social Psychology*, 53(1), pp. 5–13.

40 Russo, M. A., Santarelli, D. M. and O'Rourke, D. (2017), 'The physiological effects of slow breathing in the healthy human', *Breathe*, 13(4), pp. 298–309.

41 Brewer, J. A. et al. (2011), 'Meditation experience is associated with differences in default mode network activity and connectivity', *Proceedings of the National Academy of Sciences*, 108(50), pp. 20254–9.

42 Franklin, M. S., Mrazek, M. D., Anderson, C. L. et al. (2013), 'The silver lining of a mind in the clouds: interesting musings are associated with positive mood while mind-wandering', *Frontiers in Psychology*, 4, p. 583.

43 Bar, M. (2022), *Mindwandering: How It Can Improve Your Mood and Boost Your Creativity* (London: Bloomsbury)

44 Csikszentmihalyi, M. (1990), *Flow: The Psychology of Optimal Experience* (New York: Harper and Row)

45 Vygotsky, L. S. (1978), *Mind in Society: The Development of Higher Mental Processes* (Cambridge, MA: Harvard University Press)

46 Vygotsky, L. S. (1933), 'Play and its role in the mental development of the child', *Soviet Psychology*, 5(3), pp. 6–18.

47 Kross, E. (2021), *Chatter: The Voice in Our Head and How to Harness It* (London: Vermillion)

48 Kross, E. (2009), 'When self becomes other', *Annals of the New York Academy of Sciences*, 1167(1), pp. 35–40.

49 Orvell, A., Ayduk, Ö., Moser, J. S. et al. (2019), 'Linguistic shifts: a relatively effortless route to emotion regulation?', *Current Directions in Psychological Science*, 28(6), pp. 567–73.

50 Moser, J. S., Dougherty, A., Mattson, W. I. et al., (2017), 'Third-person self-talk facilitates emotion regulation without engaging cognitive control: converging evidence from ERP and fMRI', *Scientific Reports*, 7(1), article 4519, https://doi.org/10.1038/s41598-017-04047-3 (accessed 28 September 2023)

Lesson Six: Connect with Others

1 Leary, M. (2007), *The Curse of Self: Self-Awareness, Egotism, and the Quality of Human Life* (New York: Oxford University Press)

2 Todd, A. R., Forstmann, M., Burgmer, P. et al. (2015), 'Anxious and egocentric: how specific emotions influence perspective taking', *Journal of Experimental Psychology: General*, 144(2), pp. 374–91.

3 Rubin, K. H. and Burgess, K. (2001), 'Social withdrawal', in M. W. Vasey and M. R. Dadds (eds.), *The Developmental Psychopathology of Anxiety* (Oxford: Oxford University Press), pp. 407–34.

4 Open Access Government, 'Increased loneliness has become a global public health issue', 10 February 2022, https://www.openaccessgovernment.org/loneliness-health-countries/129381/ (accessed 13 July 2023)

5 Dahlgreen, W., 'Love thy neighbour? British people are barely friends with them', 10 September 2015, https://yougov.co.uk/topics/society/articles-reports/2015/09/10/love-thy-neighbour-british-people-are-barely-frien (accessed 28 September 2023)

6 Delhey, J., Dragolov, G. and Boehnke, K. (2023), 'Social cohesion in international comparison: a review of key

measures and findings', KZfss Kölner Zeitschrift für Soziologie und Sozialpsychologie, https://doi.org/10.1007/ s11577-023-00891-6 (accessed 28 September 2023)

7 Boothby, E. J., Clark, M. S. and Bargh, J. A. (2014), 'Shared experiences are amplified', *Psychological Science*, 25(12), pp. 2209–16.

8 Sullivan, P. and Rickers, K. (2012), 'The effect of behavioral synchrony in groups of teammates and strangers', *International Journal of Sport Exercise and Psychology*, 11(3), pp. 286–91.

9 'Overcoming the challenges of effective communication during video meetings', Hyperia, 16 August 2021, https:// hyperia.net/blog/overcoming-the-challenges-of-effective-communication-during-video-meetings (accessed 28 September 2023)

10 Jackson, J. C., Jong, J., Bilkey, D. et al. (2018), 'Synchrony and physiological arousal increase cohesion and cooperation in large naturalistic groups', *Scientific Reports*, 8, article 127, https://doi.org/10.1038/s41598-017-18023-4 (accessed 28 September 2023)

11 Cirelli, L. K., Einarson, K. M. and Trainor, L. J. (2014), 'Interpersonal synchrony increases prosocial behavior in infants', *Developmental Science*, 17(6), pp. 1003–11.

12 Reddish, P., Fischer, R. and Bulbulia, J. (2013), 'Let's dance together: synchrony, shared intentionality, and cooperation', *PLOS ONE*, 8(8), e71182, https://journals. plos.org/plosone/article?id=10.1371/journal.pone.0071182 (accessed 28 September 2023)

13 Nummenmaa, L. et al. (2012), 'Emotions promote social interaction by synchronizing brain activity across individuals', *Proceedings of the National Academy of Sciences*, 109(24), pp. 9959–604.

14 Stephens, G. J., Sibert, L. J. and Hasson, U. (2010), 'Speaker–listener neural coupling underlies successful communication', *Proceedings of the National Academy of Sciences*, 107(32), pp. 14425–30.

15 Tarr, B., Launay, J. and Dunbar, R. I. M. (2014), 'Music

and social bonding: "self-other" merging and the neurohormonal mechanisms', *Frontiers in Psychology*, 5, 1096, https://doi.org/10.3389/fpsyg.2014.01096 (accessed 28 September 2023)

16 Kreutz, G., Bongard, S., Rohrmann, S. et al. (2004), 'Effects of choir singing or listening on secretory immunoglobulin A, cortisol, and emotional state', *Journal of Behavioral Medicine*, 27(6), pp. 623–35.

17 Mogan, R., Fischer, R. and Bulbulia, J. A. (2017), 'To be in synchrony or not? A meta-analysis of synchrony's effects on behavior, perception, cognition and affect', *Journal of Experimental Social Psychology*, 72, pp. 13–20.

18 Dwyer, R. J., Kushlev, K. and Dunn, E. W. (2018), 'Smartphone use undermines enjoyment of face-to-face social interactions', *Journal of Experimental Social Psychology*, 78, pp. 233–9.

19 Baker, E. L., Dunne-Moses, A., Calarco, A. J. et al. (2019), 'Listening to understand: a core leadership skill', *Journal of Public Health Management and Practice*, 25(5), pp. 508–10.

20 Kawamichi, H., Yoshihara, K., Sasaki, A. T. et al. (2015), 'Perceiving active listening activates the reward system and improves the impression of relevant experiences', *Social Neuroscience*, 10(1), pp. 16–26.

21 Lamm, C., Decety, J. and Singer, T. (2011), 'Meta-analytic evidence for common and distinct neural networks associated with directly experienced pain and empathy for pain', *Neuroimage*, 54, pp. 2492–502.

22 Hoffman, M. L. (2002), 'How automatic and representational is empathy, and why', *Behavioural Brain Sciences*, 25(1), pp. 38–9.

23 Decety, J., Chen, C., Harenski, C. et al. (2013), 'An fMRI study of affective perspective taking in individuals with psychopathy: imagining another in pain does not evoke empathy', *Frontiers in Human Neuroscience*, https://doi.org/10.3389/fnhum.2013.00489 (accessed 28 September 2023)

24 Ward, J., Schnakenberg, P. and Banissy, M. J. (2018),

'The relationship between mirror-touch synaesthesia and empathy: new evidence and a new screening tool', *Cognitive Neuropsychology*, 35(5–6), pp. 314–32.

25 Ward, J. and Banissy, M. J. (2015), 'Explaining mirror-touch synesthesia', *Cognitive Neuroscience*, 6(2–3), pp. 118–33.

26 Singer, T. and Klimecki, O. M. (2014), 'Empathy and compassion', *Current Biology*, 24(18), pp. 875–8.

27 Dowling, T. (2018), 'Compassion does not fatigue!' *Canadian Veterinary Journal*, 59(7), pp. 749–50.

28 Skar, L. and Soderberg, S., (2018), 'Patients' complaints regarding healthcare encounters and communication', *Nursing Open*, 5(2), pp. 224–32.

29 Warrier, V., Toro, R., Chakrabarti, B. et al. (2018), 'Genome-wide analyses of self-reported empathy: correlations with autism, schizophrenia, and anorexia nervosa', *Translational Psychiatry*, 8(1), https://doi.org/10.1038/s41398-017-0082-6 (accessed 28 September 2023)

30 Melchers, M., Reuter, M., Spinath, F. M. et al. (2016), 'How heritable is empathy? Differential effects of measurement and subcomponents', *Motivation and Emotion*, 40(5), pp. 720–30.

31 Martin, G. B. and Clark, R. D. (1982), 'Distress crying in neonates: species and peer specificity', *Developmental Psychology*, 18(1), pp. 3–9.

32 Ruffman, T., Then, R., Cheng, C. et al. (2019), 'Lifespan differences in emotional contagion while watching emotion-eliciting videos', PLOS ONE, 14(1), e0209253, https://doi.org/10.1371/journal.pone.0209253 (accessed 8 November 2023)

33 Eisenberg, N. and Morris, A. S. (2001), 'The origins and social significance of empathy-related responding. A review of empathy and moral development: implications for caring and justice by M.L. Hoffman', *Social Justice Research*, 14(1), pp. 95–120.

34 Breithaupt, F. (2019), *The Dark Sides of Empathy* (Ithaca, NY: Cornell University Press)

35 Singer, T., Seymour, B., O'Doherty, J. P. et al. (2006),
    'Empathic neural responses are modulated by the
    perceived fairness of others', *Nature*, 439(7075), pp. 466–9.
36 Singer, T. and Klimecki, O. M. (2014), 'Empathy and
    compassion', *Current Biology*, 24, pp. 875–8.
37 Singer, T., Kok, B. E., Bornemann, B. et al. (2016), 'The
    ReSource Project. Background, Design, Samples, and
    Measurements (second edition)', Max Planck Institute for
    Human Cognitive and Brain Sciences.
38 Trautwein, F.-M., Kanske, P., Böckler, A. et al. (2020),
    'Differential benefits of mental training types for
    attention, compassion, and theory of mind', *Cognition*,
    194, article 104039, https://doi.org/10.1016/j.
    cognition.2019.104039 (accessed 28 September 2023)
39 Hutcherson, C. A., Seppala, E. M. and Gross, J. J.
    (2008), 'Loving-kindness meditation increases social
    connectedness', *Emotion*, 8(5), pp. 720–4.
40 Fredrickson, B. L. (2004), 'The broaden-and-build theory
    of positive emotions', *Philosophical Transactions of the
    Royal Society B*, 359(1449), pp. 1367–77.
41 Fredrickson, B. L. and Branigan, C. (2005), 'Positive
    emotions broaden the scope of attention and thought-
    action repertoires', *Cognition & Emotion*, 19(3), pp. 313–17.
42 Isen, A. M. (1993), 'Positive affect and decision making',
    in M. Lewis and J. M. Hailand-Jones (eds.), *Handbook of
    Emotions* (New York: Guilford Press), pp. 261–78.
43 Carnevale, P. J. and Isen, A. M. (1986), 'The influence
    of positive affect and visual access on the discovery
    of integrative solutions in bilateral negotiation',
    Organizational Behavior and Human Decision Processes,
    37(1), pp. 1–13.
44 Rentfrow, P. J., Jokela, M. and Lamb, M. E. (2015),
    'Regional personality differences in Great Britain', *PLOS
    ONE*, 10(3), e0122245, https://doi.org/10.1371/journal.
    pone.0122245 (accessed 28 September 2023)
45 https://www.irri.org/where-we-work/countries/china
    (accessed 28 September 2023)

Notes

46 Buck, J. L. (1935), *Land Utilization in China* (Chicago: University of Chicago Press)

47 Talhelm, T., Zhang, X., Oishi, S. et al. (2014), 'Large-scale psychological differences within China explained by rice versus wheat agriculture', *Science*, 344(6184), pp. 603–8.

48 Kitayama, S., Park, H., Sevincer, A. T. et al. (2009), 'A cultural task analysis of implicit independence: comparing North America, Western Europe, and East Asia', *Journal of Personality and Social Psychology*, 97(2), pp. 236–55.

49 Talhem., T. (2020), 'Emerging evidence of cultural differences linked to rice versus wheat agriculture', *Current Opinion in Psychology*, 32, pp. 81–8.

50 Lester, D. (1995), 'Individualism and divorce', *Psychological Reports*, 76(1), p. 258.

51 Talhelm, T., Zhang, X. and Oishi, S. (2018), 'Moving chairs in Starbucks: observational studies find rice-wheat cultural differences in daily life in China', *Science Advances*, 4(4), eaap8469, https://doi.org/ 10.1126/sciadv. aap8 (accessed 28 September 2023)

52 Talhelm, T. (2022), 'The rice theory of culture', *Online Readings in Psychology and Culture*, 4(1), https://doi. org/10.9707/2307-0919.1172 (accessed 8 November 2023)

53 Mesoudi, A., Magid, K. and Hussain, D. (2016), 'How do people become W.E.I.R.D.? Migration reveals the cultural transmission mechanisms underlying variation in psychological processes', *PLOS ONE*, 11(1), e0147162, https://doi.org/10.1371/journal.pone.0147162 (accessed 28 September 2023)

54 Buss, D. M. (2005), *The Murderer Next Door: Why the Mind is Designed to Kill* (New York: Penguin)

55 Van Lier, J., Revlin, R. and De Neys, W. (2013), 'Detecting cheaters without thinking: testing the automaticity of the cheater detection module', *PLOS ONE*, 8(1), e53827, https://doi.org/10.1371/journal.pone.0053827 (accessed 8 November 2023)

56 Fehr, E. and Gächter, S. (2002), 'Altruistic punishment in humans', *Nature*, 415(6868), pp. 137–40.

57 Putnam, R. (2000), *Bowling Alone: The Collapse and Revival of American Community* (New York: Simon & Schuster)

58 Delhey, J. and Welzel, C. (2012), 'Generalizing trust: how outgroup-trust grows beyond ingroup trust', *World Values Research*, 5(3), pp. 46–69.

59 Martela, F., Greve, B., Rothstein, B. et al. (2020), 'The Nordic exceptionalism: what explains why the Nordic countries are constantly among the happiest in the world' in *World Happiness Report 2020,* https://worldhappiness.report/ed/2020/the-nordic-exceptionalism-what-explains-why-the-nordic-countries-are-constantly-among-the-happiest-in-the-world/ (accessed 8 November 2023)

60 Cohn., A., Maréchat, M. A., Tennebaum, D. et al. (2019), 'Civic honesty around the globe', *Science*, 365(6448), pp. 70–3.

61 Helliwell, J. F., Layard, R. and Sachs, J. (2013), *World Happiness Report 2013*, https://worldhappiness.report/ed/2013/ (accessed 28 September 2023)

62 https://bemoreus.org.uk/video (accessed 28 September 2023)

63 Ebbesen, E. B., Kjos, G. L. and Konecni, V. J. (1976), 'Spatial ecology: its effects on the choice of friends and enemies', *Journal of Experimental Social Psychology*, 12(6), pp. 505–18.

64 'Londoners launch anti-Tube Chat campaign', BBC News, 30 September 2016, https://www.bbc.co.uk/news/uk-england-london-37521090 (accessed 28 September 2023)

65 Grierson, J., '"Tube Chat" campaign provokes horror among London commuters', *The Guardian*, 29 September 2016, https://www.theguardian.com/uk-news/2016/sep/29/tube-chat-campaign-provokes-horror-among-london-commuters (accessed 28 September 2023)

66 Smith, M., 'It's good to talk? Not if you're young or on public transport', YouGov, 12 December 2017, https://www.yougov.co.uk/topics/politics/articles-reports/2017/12/12/

its-good-talk-one-four-brits-would-prefer-not-talk (accessed 28 September 2023)

67 Pan, J. (2019), *Sorry I'm Late, I Didn't Want to Come: An Introvert's Year of Living Dangerously* (New York: Doubleday)

68 Epley, N. and Schroeder, J. (2014), 'Mistakenly seeking solitude', *Journal of Experimental Psychology: General*, 143(5), pp. 1980–99.

69 Schroeder, J., Lyons, D. and Epley, N. (2022), 'Hello, stranger? Pleasant conversations are preceded by concerns about starting one', *Journal of Experimental Psychology: General*, 151(5), pp. 1141–53.

70 Miller, D. T. and McFarland, C. (1991), 'When social comparison goes awry; the case of pluralistic ignorance', in J. Suls and T. Wils (eds.), *Social Comparison: Contemporary Theory and Research* (Hillsdale, NJ: Erlbaum)

71 Boothby, B. J., 'The liking gap in conversations: do people like us more than we think?', *Psychological Science*, 29(11), pp. 1742–56.

72 Gilovich, T., Medvec, V. H. and Savitsky, K. (2000), 'The spotlight effect in social judgment: an egocentric bias in estimates of the salience of one's own actions and appearance', *Journal of Personality and Social Psychology*, 78(2), pp. 211–22.

Lesson Seven: Get Out of Your Own Head

1 Minutaglio, B. and Davis, S. L. (2018), *The Most Dangerous Man in America: Timothy Leary, Richard Nixon and the Hunt for the Fugitive King of LSD* (New York: Grand Central Publishing)

2 Dos Santos, R., Osorio, F. L., Crippa, J. A. S. et al. (2017), 'Anxiety, panic, and hopelessness during and after ritual ayahuasca intake in a woman with generalized anxiety disorder: a case report', *Journal of Psychedelic Studies*, 1(1), pp. 35–9.

3 Aday, J. S., Davis, A. K., Mitzkovitz, C. M. et al. (2021),

'Predicting reactions to psychedelic drugs: a systematic review of states and traits related to acute drug effects', *ACS Pharmacology & Translational Science*, 4(2), pp. 424–35.

4 Davis, A. K., Barrett, F. S., May, D. G. et al. (2021), 'Effects of psilocybin-assisted therapy on major depressive disorder: a randomized clinical trial', *JAMA Psychiatry*, 78(5), pp. 481–89.

5 Devlin, H., 'Psychedelic drug research held back by UK rules and and attitudes, say scientists', 8 November 2022, https://www.theguardian.com/science/2022/nov/08/psilocybin-research-kept-in-limbo-by-rules-and-attitudes-say-scientists (accessed 8 November 2023)

6 Ollove, M., 'More states may legalize psychedelic mushrooms', Stateline, 15 July 2022, https://www.pewtrusts.org/en/research-and-analysis/blogs/stateline/2022/07/15/more-states-may-legalize-psychedelic-mushrooms

7 Tagliazucci, E., Roseman, L., Kaelen, M. et al. (2016), 'Increased global functional connectivity correlates with LSD-induced ego dissolution', *Current Biology*, 26(8), pp. 1043–50.

8 Hood, B. (2012), *The Self Illusion: Why There is No 'You' Inside Your Head* (London: Constable & Robinson)

9 Griffiths, R. R., Hurwitz, E. S., Davis, A. K. et al. (2019), 'Survey of subjective "God encounter experiences": comparisons among naturally occurring experiences and those occasioned by the classic psychedelics psilocybin, LSD, ayahuasca, or DMT', *PLOS ONE*, 14(4), e0214377, https://journals.plos.org/plosone/article?id=10.1371/journal.pone.0214377 (accessed 8 November 2023)

10 Pearce, E., Launay, J. and Dunbar, R. I. M. (2015), 'The ice-breaker effect: singing mediates fast social bonding', *Royal Society Open Science*, 2(1), article 150221, https://doi.org/10.1098/rsos.15022 1 (accessed 8 November 2023)

11 Tarr, B., Launay, J. and Dunbar, R. I. M. (2014), 'Music and social bonding: "self-other" merging and neurohormonal mechanisms', *Frontiers in Psychology*, 5, article 1096,

Notes

https://doi.org/10.3389/fpsyg.2014.01096 (accessed 8
November 2023)

12 Aaron, A., Aron, E. N. and Smollan, D. (1992),
'Inclusion of Other in the Self Scale and the structure
of interpersonal closeness', *Journal of Personality & Social
Psychology*, 63(4), pp. 596–612.

13 Greater Good in Action, https://ggia.berkeley.edu/

14 Piff, P. K., Feinberg, M., Dietze, P. et al. (2015), 'Awe, the
small self, and prosocial behavior', *Journal of Personality
and Social Psychology*, 108(6), pp. 883–99.

15 Yaden, D. B., Iwry, J., Slack, K. J. et al. (2016), 'The
overview effect: awe and self-transcendent experience in
space flight', *Psychology of Consciousness: Theory, Research,
and Practice*, 3(1), pp. 1–11.

16 van Elk, M., Karinen, A., Specker, A. et al (2016),
'"Standing in awe": the effects of awe on body perception
and the relation with absorption', *Collabra*, 2(1), pp. 1–16.

17 Sturm, V. E., Datta, S., Roy, A. R. K. et al. (2022). Big
smile, small self: Awe walks promote prosocial positive
emotions in older adults. *Emotion*, 22(5), 1044–1058.

18 Chouinard, M. M. (2007), 'Children's questions: a
mechanism for cognitive development', *Monographs for
the Society for Research in Child Development*, 72, pp. 1–129;
Sturm, V. E., Datta, S., Roy, A. R. K. et al. (2022), 'Big
smile, small self: Awe walks promote prosocial positive
emotions in older adults', *Emotion*, 22(5), pp. 1044–58.

19 Feynman, R. (1983), 'Magnets (and Why?): Fun to imagine
4', YouTube, https://www.youtube.com/watch?v=wMFPe-
DwULM (accessed 17 July 2023)

20 Popova, M. (n.d.), 'Rilke on the lonely patience of creative
work', The Marginalian, https://www.themarginalian.
org/2018/06/22/rilke-patience-solitude-art/ (accessed 8
November 2023)

21 Yaden, D. B. and Newberg, A. B. (2022), *The Varieties of
Spiritual Experience: 21st Century Research and Perspectives*
(New York: Oxford University Press)

22 Dambrun, M. (2017), 'Self-centeredness and selflessness:

happiness correlates and mediating psychological processes', *PeerJ*, 5, e3306, https://doi.org/10.7717/peerj.3306 (accessed 8 November 2023)

23 Dambrun, M. and Ricard, M. (2011), 'Self-centeredness and selflessness: a theory of self-based psychological functioning and its consequences for happiness', *Review of General Psychology*, 15(2), pp. 138–57.

24 Csikszentmihalyi, M. and Hunter, J. (2003), 'Happiness in everyday life: the uses of experience sampling', *Journal of Happiness Studies: An Interdisciplinary Forum on Subjective Well-Being*, 4(2), pp. 185–99.

25 Conner, T. S., DeYoung, C. G. and Silvia, P. J. (2018), 'Everyday creative activity as a path to flourishing', *Journal of Positive Psychology*, 13(2), pp. 181–9.

26 Dobat, A. S. (2020), 'Archaeology as therapy: the metal detector hobby and mental health in Denmark', *Archaeological Forum*, 43, pp. 11–24.

INDEX

Page references in *italics* indicate images.

Index

Index

Index